Terry Barron's No Nonsense

Guide To Fly Fishing
Pyramid Lake

A Quick, Clear Understanding of the Nation's Top Lahontan Cutthroat Trout Fishery

Edited and With a Foreword by Jeff Cavender

Published by David Communications ● 6171 Tollgate, Sisters, Oregon 97759

Acknowledgments

*A*fter considerable thought about all the people that helped me with this book, I realized what an extremely fortunate person I am. I'm very lucky to have these people, and many more, to thank.

First I'd like to thank Jeff and Rebecca Cavender, two of my closest friends. Their computer and personal time got this book to completion. Secondly, I thank Dave Stanley, one the most talented and knowledgeable fly fisherman and all-around outdoorsman I know. He's allowed me to tie flies for and work in the Reno Fly Shop earning money doing what I enjoy most...fly fishing.

Next I thank the following people who have helped in countless ways: Richard Dickerson for his photos and his company on the many freezing mornings he's gone fishing with me, Ann and Ron Privrasky and Ron Anfinson for their help with photos and the fly plate, and especially Paul Wagner, former Director of Pyramid Lake Fisheries, and Nancy Vucinich, acting Resource Manager of Pyramid Lake Fisheries for their unselfish help, time, facts and charts.

I also appreciate the gracious contribution of flies from Glenn Allred, Ike Berry, Doug Ouellette, Dave Stanley and Mark Tilton. Thanks to Bud Johnson, Sash Nakamoto, Alan Seelye, Tom Bradshaw and David Baba for their support and inspiration and to Teresa Centrella-Weeks who loaned her portable computer. Further thanks go to David Banks, the publisher, who never lost faith in me and William "Woody" Woodruff, an excellent fly fisherman and perfectionist fly tier who taught me proper fly tying. Also, my thanks to my good friends of many years: Jim Conyne, Tony Lee, Lee Nielsen, Kurt Sieben and Bruce Wagoner. All have spent many miserably cold, windy days (with a few warm times) casting for hours on end for giant Pyramid Lake trout.

Many people have contributed to the rebirth of Pyramid's fishery and are mentioned in the ensuing chapters. Credit must be given here to biologists Thomas Trelease and Kay Johnson. In the late 1940's, together with Ira La Rivers, they labored heroically to restore trout to Pyramid when the popular belief was that trout couldn't survive in the lake. Their optimism and determination lives in many of us today.

Sincere thanks goes to the Paiute people of Pyramid Lake. Their generosity and efforts enable us to continue enjoying a beautiful and productive fishery. The Pyramid Lake Paiute Tribe has spent millions of dollars to keep their fishery populated with true Lahontan cutthroat for all to enjoy.

Finally, I acknowledge John Champion. This native Nevadan and Reno resident was the Cal Trout stream keeper for the Nevada side of the Truckee River until his untimely death in 1997. John lived up to his last name, lobbying to force the Army Corps of Engineers to honor their commitment to replace the nonfunctioning, wooden fish ladder at Derby Dam with one built of concrete. Unfortunately, the federal government claims the cost to correct the ladder is now too high.

The good news is that today, when I fish Pyramid Lake, I'm overwhelmed when I think of all the time and effort—past and present—expended by so many to give new life to one of the most beautiful trophy trout lakes in the world. Truly, the restoration of this unique fishery has been a gift to us all.

Terry Barron

Terry Barron's No Nonsense Guide To Fly Fishing Pyramid Lake
©1998 David Communications
ISBN #0-9637256-3-7

Published by David Communications
6171 Tollgate • Sisters, Oregon 97759

Printed by Patterson Printing, Benton Harbor, Michigan

Author: Terry Barron
Maps, Cover & Illustrations: Pete Chadwell
Proofing: Adrienne Banks

Editors: Jeff Cavender, David Banks
Production & Art Direction: Aprille Chadwell
Front & Back Cover Photos: Richard Dickerson, Terry Barron, David Banks

David Communications believes that in addition to local information and gear, fly fishers need fresh water and healthy fish. The publisher encourages preservation, improvement, conservation, enjoyment and understanding of our waters and their inhabitants. A good way to do this is to support organizations dedicated to these ideas.

David Communications is a member and sponsor of, and donor to Trout Unlimited, The Federation of Fly Fishers, Oregon Trout, California Trout, New Mexico Trout, Amigos Bravos, North American Fly-Tackle Trade Association, American Rivers, Waterfowl U.S.A. and Ducks Unlimited. We encourage you to get involved, learn more and to join such organizations.
  • Trout Unlimited 1(800) 834-2419 • Federation of Fly Fishers (406) 585-7592 • Oregon Trout (503) 222-9091
  • California Trout (415) 392-8887 • New Mexico Trout (505) 344-6363 • Amigos Bravos (505) 758-3874
  • Waterfowl U.S.A. • American Rivers (202) 547-6900 • Ducks Unlimited (901) 758-3825.

Disclaimer - While this guide will greatly help readers to fly fish, it is not a substitute for caution, good judgement and the services of a qualified guide or outfitter.

Manufactured in the United States of America

*This book is dedicated to my family.
My wife, Lorraine, for her 25 years of love, support and inspiration that give me the chance to do many things and go many places. My father, Albert Barron, who introduced me to fly fishing for bluegills at age six. To my departed mother, Lois McCoy-Barron, who gave me permission to pursue fishing and hunting, even at a young age.*

PYRAMID LAKE, NEVADA

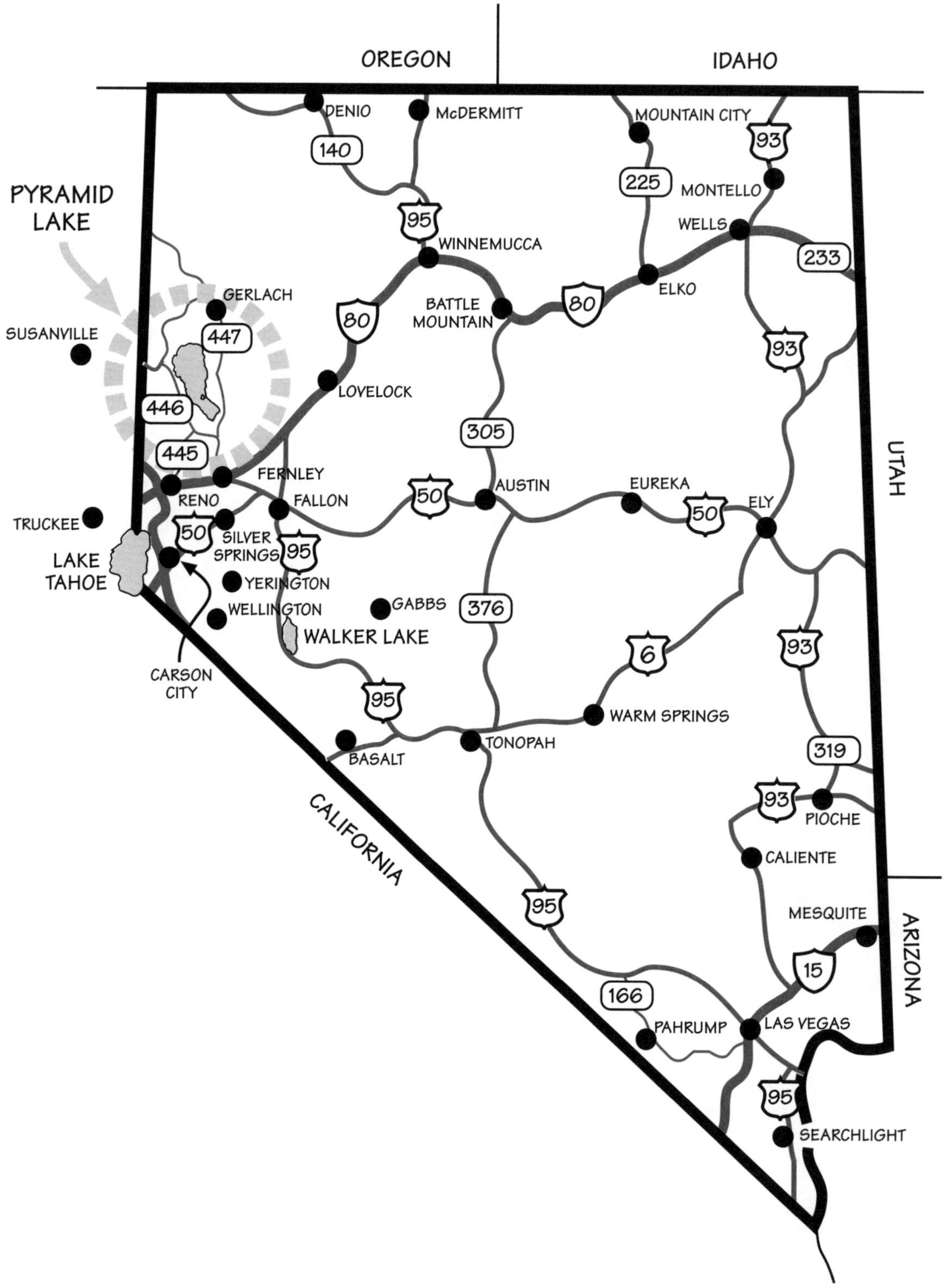

OREGON

IDAHO

DENIO

McDERMITT

MOUNTAIN CITY

140

93

95

225

MONTELLO

WINNEMUCCA

WELLS

PYRAMID
LAKE

GERLACH

80

BATTLE
MOUNTAIN

80

ELKO

233

SUSANVILLE

447

93

446

LOVELOCK

445

FERNLEY

305

RENO

FALLON

AUSTIN

EUREKA

ELY

TRUCKEE

50

50

50

LAKE
TAHOE

SILVER
SPRINGS

95

YERINGTON

WELLINGTON

GABBS

376

93

WALKER LAKE

6

CARSON
CITY

95

WARM SPRINGS

BASALT

TONOPAH

319

CALIFORNIA

93

PIOCHE

CALIENTE

MESQUITE

ARIZONA

95

15

166

PAHRUMP

LAS VEGAS

95

SEARCHLIGHT

UTAH

Contents

Foreword

Thoughts on fly fishing, Pyramid Lake & the author
from a native Nevadan

When I began casting a fly rod twenty-six years ago, there weren't many good sources of information. No Scientific Angler fly fishing videos, no library of "little books" by Lefty Kreh that revealed the secrets of the sport to subscribers... no upscale fly shops staffed by FFF Certified Casting Instructors in every town close to a fishable water. My apprenticeship in fly fishing was the result of the generosity of a series of more experienced anglers who blessed me with fishing secrets they spent a lifetime gathering. Maybe it was because I always listened carefully and respectfully to what they passed down to me. Maybe they shared their knowledge because I knew to bring the lunch and beer if I was fortunate enough to be invited to come along. Maybe it was because I never killed a fish or revealed the location of any new fishing spot they took me to. Or perhaps it was because they recognized that my interest in fly fishing was a desire to change the way I fished and not just a calculated attempt to catch more fish.

Like many other fishermen, indeed, like most of my fly fishing mentors, I spent years bait casting and spin fishing before I was drawn to the aesthetics of angling with a fly. During those years, I came to understand that the fortunate days I spent on a river or stillwater were more about being "out there" than they were about merely catching fish. Crisp mornings spent watching swallows work a Callibaetis hatch on a small desert reservoir, afternoons spent turning over rocks in a cold, clear stream to catch a glimpse of the incredible world living there, and evenings where the sunset was so beautiful my casting arm actually stopped working. These were natural extensions of this growing understanding, an understanding and appreciation which eventually drew me exclusively to the graceful rhythms of casting the long rod.

In many respects, today's beginning fly anglers have lost a great deal, as has the sport itself. Videos, books and magazines, and the proliferation of highly skilled pro shops and schools have done away with the apprenticeship system of a few years ago.

While any angler wants to hook up, it seems our streams and lakes are now beset by legions of well-equipped, well-schooled anglers who just want to catch fish. They have not undergone the evolutionary process that emphasizes "how" and not "how many" that, at one time, the journeyman demanded of the apprentice.

Though only a few years older than I, Terry Barron was, and is, one of my journeyman mentors. But it's not just because he taught me how to manufacture a well-tied fly or introduced me to the Junkyard Pool on the Truckee River. In fact, Terry's basic decency, generosity, and good humor have taught me as much about being a better human being as his fly tying and fishing expertise has taught me about being a proficient angler.

Pyramid Lake is just one of the great fly fishing waters Terry has introduced me to. I can't think of a fishery better suited to test the evolved temperament of a fly angler. Pyramid does have those days when anyone can catch fish, even a lot of fish, and even a trophy fish. But many more days the lake demands the best of an angler, then sends him or her home without even a "bump."

This is not to say that Pyramid is a selfish brute, totally unmindful of the implied "give-and-take" of the angling process. Anyone who has witnessed the rosy-orange of late afternoon illuminate "The Pyramid" or waded out over the lake's clean, sand bottom into its turquoise waters to cast a fly has not come away empty handed. These are gifts reserved for anglers who have learned that "there is a lot more to fly fishing than catching fish," gifts that Terry Barron and Pyramid Lake have given me.

This book, Terry's first, is an attempt to give you many of these gifts. The only thing you won't get from this guide is the pleasure of having Terry there fishing with you and providing humor and patient instruction.

Jeff Cavender
Reno, Nevada
December, 1997

Preface

The "pyramid" on the east shore of Pyramid Lake. John C. Fremont, while exploring the area with Kit Carson, named the tufa formation in 1844.
Photo: Terry Barron

*M*y first experience with Pyramid Lake was a brief, unscheduled visit on an overcast day in November, 1963. I'd skipped a day of high school. Since returning home to face my mother didn't seem like the best plan, I decided to take a drive north of town to a lake I'd overheard some fishermen talking about. Nothing I'd overheard could have prepared me for my first view of this unbelievable body of water located, it seemed, in the middle of nowhere. It was huge. Many different shades of blue played against the stark, foreboding shoreline. Although I only looked around for a few minutes, my first sight of this magnificent, magical scene sent a chill down my spine. Back then, however, it was one thing to skip school and another to be late for dinner. I reluctantly headed back to town, haunted by what I had seen. It wouldn't be until after high school, and a two-year sidetrip to southeast Asia, before I returned to the lake that had effected me so on that dark, November day.

My second experience with the lake was after the Army in 1971 when I moved back to Reno. I was tying my own flies by this time though my efforts were mostly standard dry and nymph patterns such as the Adams and Gold Ribbed Hare's Ear I used on the small streams of the western Sierra.

I didn't have an idea in the world what patterns to tie for Pyramid Lake, so I purchased some flies recommended by a local sporting goods store and drove to the lake. Not knowing a thing about where or how to fish, I chose a place on the western shoreline where a small snow-melt stream entered, tied on a Olive Woolly Worm with grizzly hackle and a red tail and began casting. I can't remember how many casts I made that first day, but I did manage to land an eighteen inch fish.

Although I fished the lake several more times that year without catching another fish, I knew that one fish, small by Pyramid Lake standards, had hooked me as surely as I had hooked it. Over years of fishing Pyramid, my fishless frustration turned to determination. I began to tie better flies and use them with better casting and fishing techniques. I learned to feel the bottom with my fly and discovered that moving to different areas rather than staying in the same spot for hours at a time usually yielded more fish.

It seemed to me at the time (and still does) that the amount of bad information about Pyramid is almost directly proportional to the size of the lake. I learned that one of the hardest lessons to learn about fishing Pyramid was distinguishing between good and bad advice, between mere rumor and fact. This took me years to learn and is largely the reason I decided to write a book about fly fishing this beautiful desert lake.

In these pages, you will not find the entire history of Pyramid Lake and the people who believe the lake to be sacred, the Paiute Indian people (pronounced Pi-yut). I have, however, included some limited historical perspective. If you are interested in more Pyramid Lake history I recommend any of the excellent books available on the subject. Two of which— *The Desert Lake, the Story of Nevada's Pyramid Lake* by Sessions S. Wheeler and *Fishes and Fisheries of Nevada* by Ira La Rivers—I highly recommend.

Pyramid Lake has been called the most beautiful desert lake in North America. First time visitors should take the time to travel around the lake, maybe even spending the night to properly experience the lake's many moods and colors. Impressed or not, all visitors should show respect for the lake and the people who love it. Here are two primary areas of concern.

First and most importantly, anyone caught littering should be subject to the harshest punishment or fine possible. It's incomprehensible to me that someone blessed with the time to enjoy a naturally beautiful setting such as Pyramid Lake would show their gratitude by leaving behind a soiled diaper or a pile of empty beer cans.

Secondly, catch & release anglers should know how to properly handle fish. I advocate this because it gives the fish and the lake their best chance to reach maximum potential. The theory of catch & release, however, does little good if the practitioners don't know what they are doing. Anglers lucky enough to be fishing on one of those magical days when the fish are hitting constantly, should play them quickly and be especially gentle when releasing them. Never kick fish up on the bank to weigh or measure them, as many ignorant anglers still do. Know how to properly photograph and release fish: keep them submerged in water until ready to photograph and then make sure they have been completely revived before release.

If you need to keep fish, abide by the slot and creel limits set by the Pyramid Lake Piaute Tribe, who own and manage the lake. These limits provide hatchery spawned fish the best chance to survive when returned to the water and, consequently, a better chance to spawn a second time. If you must, quickly kill the fish by hitting it sharply between their eyes with a heavy object. Why cause needless suffering on the end of a stringer. As a friend once put it, "Keeping a fish alive on a stringer is like choking a friendly dog."

Over the years, the Paiute people of Pyramid Lake have spent countless hours and dollars lobbying to regain some of the tribe's original water rights on the Truckee River, the most important source of water for Pyramid Lake. Over the last hundred years or so, it has been one of the most abused rivers in the country. Only in the last couple of decades has there has been some changes in the allocation of water from the Truckee. This is attributable, for the most part, to the perseverance of the Pyramid Lake Piaute Tribe. Because of the tribe's efforts, five pound fish are still very common in Pyramid Lake, and many ten pound and larger fish are caught annually.

Even so, the Pyramid Lake Paiute Tribe can only do so much. Legislated river flows, for certain times of the year, will certainly help to keep Pyramid's water level from falling as it has in the past, but ultimately, only Mother Nature can *ensure* the lake's future.

The winters of 1995-1998 have brought the eastern Sierra some of the heaviest snowfalls on record, and Pyramid Lake is now approaching its highest water levels since the 1940's. With this inflow of fresh water, the lake's aquatic life, from lowly plankton to the majestic Lahontan Cutthroat, has dramatically rebounded. Let us hope this cycle continues.

The author, with evidence he has learned to distinguish the good Pyramid Lake fly fishing advice from the bad.
Photo: David Banks

A No Nonsense Display of
Common Fish
In Pyramid Lake and the Truckee River

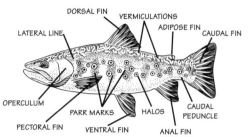

Typical trout, salmon or char.

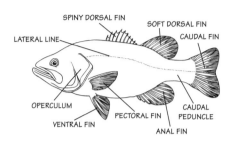

Typical bass, perch, crappie.

LAHONTAN CUTTHROAT TROUT

Red or orange mark under jaws. Brownish green colored back, large black spots on tail decreasing in number towards head. Red-orange or rose colored on sides and pink or yellow underneath.

RAINBOW TROUT

The most abundant wild and hatchery fish. An olive-bluish back with small black spots. Sides have light red or pink band. Lake 'bows are often all silver.

ASIATIC CARP

Similar to catfish and chub. Medium olive color on back, yellowish on sides, sometimes red tint on fins, rough scales and small whiskers. Introduced into Pyramid Lake in late 1800's as possible food source.

SACRAMENTO PERCH

Overall green-purple metallic color. Back is bluish-white to brown. Black mottles and vertical bars on sides, belly silver, black dot on gill covers. Spawn near rocks in fall. Introduced in Pyramid Lake in 1880 as possible sportfish and food source.

BROWN TROUT

Brown colored back with big black spots. A square tail and black and red spots on sides with light blue rings. Hard to catch, easily spooked.

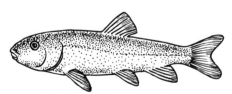

CUI-UI or LAKE SUCKER

Male back black to brownish with reddish sides. Female bluish-gray cast. Feed in depths of 30' - 100' on small invertebrates, insects. Can live up to 18 years, grow to 16 lbs.

TUI CHUB

Main baitfish of Pyramid cutthroat. Back olive colored, sides light olive and belly white and yellow. Fins tinted with red. Live up to 7 years and grow to 16".

Illustrations by Pete Chadwell. For fine art and fish renderings write to:
Dynamic Arts 1832 N.E. Providence Dr. • Bend, OR 97701.

A No Nonsense Display of
The Best Flies To Use in Pyramid Lake

BLACK/CHARTREUSE WOOLLY WORM

BLACK/RED WOOLLY WORM

BLACK/BLUE WOOLLY WORM

OLIVE/GRIZZLY WOOLLY WORM

PURPLE PEARL WING WOOLLY WORM

RAINBOW/BLACK WOOLLY WORM

WHITE/WHITE WOOLLY WORM

DAVE WHITLOCK'S DRAGON NYMPH

DAVE STANLEY'S DRAGON NYMPH

NEALLEY'S DRAGON NYMPH

IKE BERRY'S FOAM BEETLE

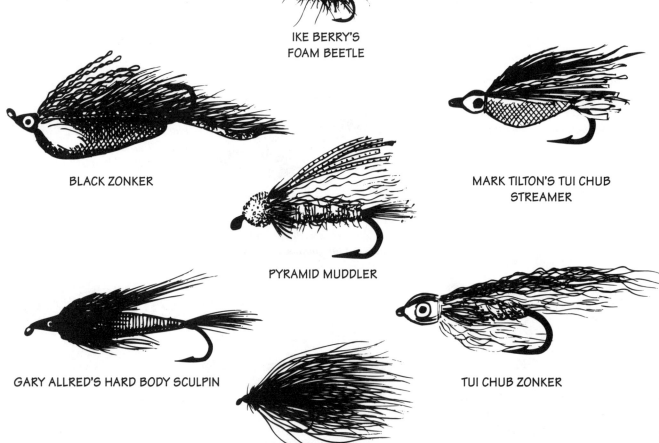

BLACK ZONKER

MARK TILTON'S TUI CHUB STREAMER

PYRAMID MUDDLER

GARY ALLRED'S HARD BODY SCULPIN

TUI CHUB ZONKER

DOUG OULLETTE'S SPIDER FLY

Illustrations by Pete Chadwell. For fine art and fish renderings write to: Pete Chadwell •1832 N.E. Providence Dr. • Bend, OR 97701.

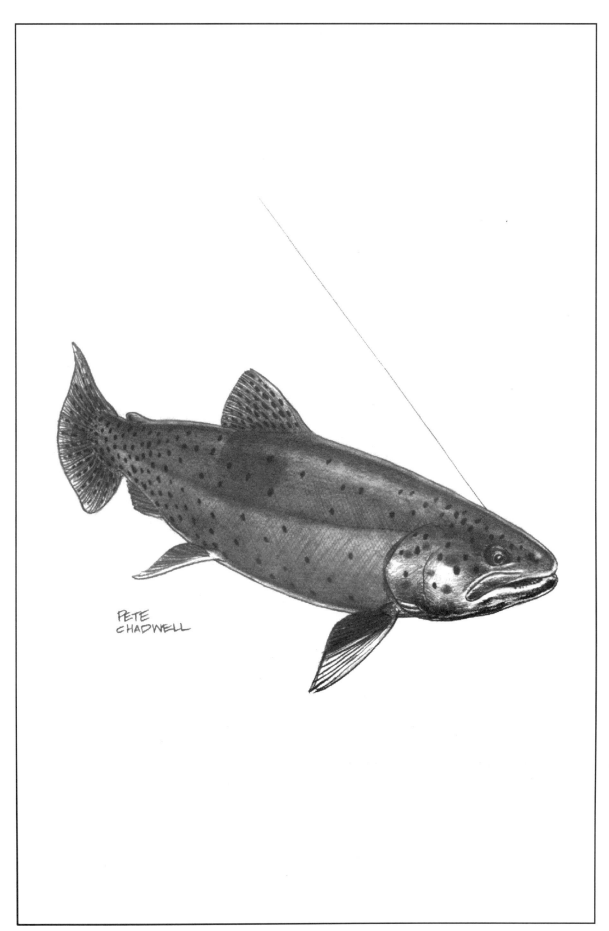

Lahontan Cutthroat Trout

Pyramid Lake Chronology

A quick history. More than you thought you'd like to know about this huge lake.

Permian Period - 200,000,000 B.C.
Shallow marine waters cover what is now Nevada. Large Sharks inhabit these waters.

Cretaceous Period - 120,000,000 B.C.
First relatives of modern Lahontan Cutthroat present. Remains have been found in rocks of east-central Nevada.

Miocene Period - 20,000,000 B.C.
First relatives of the modern sucker fish present.

Pleistocene Period - 50,000 B.C.
Fragments of modern day fish deposited, including cutthroat, Tui Chub, Lake Sucker.

10,000 B.C.
Evidence Indians of the Lovelock Cave Culture (near Humboldt sink) living on fish.

1300 - 1400's
Modern day Paiutes established at Pyramid Lake.

1825-26
Peter Ogden, Jim Bridger other mountain men fur trapping in Nevada. Bridger hikes from the San Francisco area, across central Nevada to Salt Lake.

1833
"Kit" Carson possibly first white man to see Pyramid Lake. Names it Mary's Lake.

1843
John C. Fremont and Kit Carson explore Nevada.

1844
Fremont and Carson discover Pyramid Lake, January 10. Believe it Mary's Lake (i.e., Humboldt Sink). Fremont names Pyramid after large triangular shaped tufa formation. Names river flowing into south end Salmon Trout River.

Caleb Greenwood, 81 year old mountain man, guides immigrants up Salmon Trout River, across North Pass, later called Donner Pass. Greenwood Party names river Truckee, after Indian who directed them. Name prevails. Lake at North Pass trail called Truckee, changed to Donner Lake.

1875-77
David Star Jordan, Theodore Gilland, H.W. Henshaw collect, describe, report on fish, including Salmo Clarki - Henshawi, Lahontan Cutthroat Trout from Lake Tahoe.

1878
H.G. Parker, first Nevada Fish Commissioner, plants Sacramento Perch in Nevada. Wants carp available for every dinner table in state.

1887
W.M. Carey succeeds Parker. Demonstrates damage sawdust mills on upper Truckee cause fish and impact of dams on lower Truckee.

1905
Derby Dam completed on Truckee river. Diverts water to valley.

1909
Crawfish and Salmon flies from Oregon planted in Truckee. Flies called Junebugs by locals.

1940
Last of original Pyramid Lake Cutthroat.

1948-49
Studies by Ira LaRivers and Tom Trelease prompt stocking of Pyramid Lake with Kokanee, Walker Lake strain Lahontan Cutthroat and Rainbows.

1960
Nevada Dept. of Fish & Game plants Cuttbows in Pyramid Lake. Fish grow fast are strong, good fighters and popular with anglers.

1974
Nevada Dept. of Wildlife stops managing Pyramid Lake. Stocking true strain Lahontan begins.

1982-83
Genetic studies verify Summit Lake strain Cutthroat are pure strain Lahontan Cutthroat. Debate continues: are they exact strain as pre-1940 fish?

1995-97
Three very wet winters in western Nevada. Pyramid Lake reaches highest level since 1940's.

Lake Lahontan

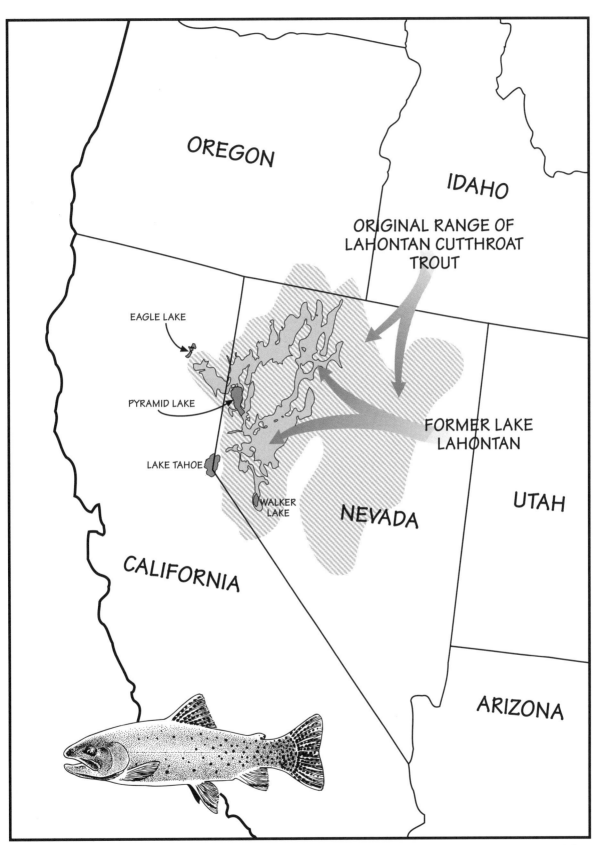

OREGON

IDAHO

ORIGINAL RANGE OF
LAHONTAN CUTTHROAT
TROUT

EAGLE LAKE

PYRAMID LAKE

LAKE TAHOE

WALKER
LAKE

FORMER LAKE
LAHONTAN

NEVADA

UTAH

CALIFORNIA

ARIZONA

Over 120,000,000 years ago the geology of most of Nevada allowed for a giant, shallow lake. It is believed the Lahontan cutthroat trout evolved in these waters. It's rather amazing to consider the Pyramid cutthroat you hook today once developed in and ranged over such a vast expanse.

Pyramid Lake & Its Trout

Fly fishing Pyramid Lake can be arduous and the landscape seemingly barren. The rewards, however, can be great and the scene inspiring. This angler is casting from the west shore towards the "pyramid", about seven miles away. Even shooting head lines won't reach it.
Photo: Richard Dickerson.

*F*ly fishing Pyramid Lake is often demanding: fighting the elements and casting for hours while controlling the hope of catching a trophy cutthroat on a fly. These demands are also a good portion of the attraction of the place. I want the techniques in these pages to help every angler's quest to hook a giant Pyramid cutthroat. I also hope to instill an enthusiasm and affection for this ancient and mysterious lake.

Seeing Pyramid Lake and surroundings for the first time feels like stumbling upon some prehistoric landscape. Visitors and even area residents often feel this way. A little geologic history helps explain what you are seeing, and hopefully, helps you appreciate it.

The Huge Ancient Lake

Approximately 70,000 years ago an inland sea covered much of northwestern Nevada, southern Oregon and northeastern California. During its highest water years, Lake Lahontan, as it came to be called, covered an area of more than 80,000 square miles. Today, several relatively small lakes remain as evidence of that once great inland sea. Among them are Eagle Lake in northeastern California, Walker Lake in west central Nevada, and about 100 miles north of Walker, the desert jewel known as Pyramid Lake.

The Lake is entirely within the boundaries of the Pyramid Lake Paiute Indian Reservation. Located in Washoe County, Nevada it is approximately 30 miles north of the cities of Reno and Sparks. The lake's primary source of water is the Truckee River whose headwater is Lake Tahoe. The Truckee flows north-northeast 115 miles, while dropping approximately 2,432 feet by the time it reaches Pyramid.

At its present level, the lake is about 25 miles long, 4 to 11 miles wide, with a depth of over 300 feet. It's considered by many to be one of the most beautiful desert lakes in North America. While there is no disputing the lake's beauty, it's not scenery that brings an ever increasing number of people to Pyramid Lake. It is, rather, a chance to fish its clear, turquoise-blue water for the legendary Lahontan Cutthroat.

Where Pyramid Fish Used to Spawn

The events that led up to the demise of the Lahontan Cutthroat in Pyramid Lake is an interesting story. I have condensed these events in the following environmental history to give insight into how man (particularly white man) can be his own worst enemy.

Historically, from October to May, massive schools of large cutthroat made their annual migration from Pyramid Lake up the Truckee. In his book, *Fish and Fisheries of Nevada*, Ira LaRivers writes that the Paiute Indians called these fish "Tomoo-agaih" (Winter Trout). Sessions S. Wheeler, in his book, *The Desert Lake, the Story of Nevada's Pyramid Lake*, claims the Paiutes called these fish "Hoopagaih." White men of the time simply referred to them as "redfish." Today, many would call this fish a "spawner."

Records from the turn of the century show 9 to 10 pound fish were common. Twenty pounders didn't even cause much excitement. These larger redfish would usually travel no further upriver than the town of Verdi on the Nevada/California border, a distance of 50 river miles. Most would spawn in the first 30 miles

From April to June, a smaller cutthroat, which

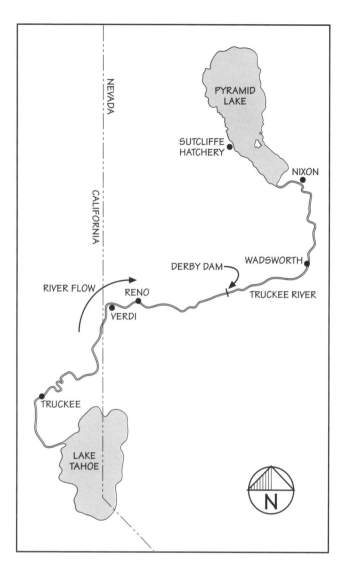

When fish went on spawning runs from Pyramid, they went about 50 miles up the Truckee River to what is now the California / Nevada border.

La Rivers and Wheeler agree the Paiutes called "Tamaagaih" (Spring Trout), would begin their journey up the Truckee River. Their migration overlapped the larger redfish. These smaller fish or "Tommies," as white men called them, would travel up and spawn along almost the entire length of the Truckee River. Unfortunately, this made them fair game to Californians as well as Nevadans.

Commercial Harvest

For decades, during their spawning migrations, redfish and tommies came under intense commercial harvesting with (surprisingly) no apparent effect on their population. From the 1860's to the 1930's Pyramid Lake was considered an inexhaustible source of Lahontan cutthroat trout. Commercial net fisherman removed tons of fish from the lake and the Truckee River. Using efficient steel gaff hooks supplied by the white man, the Paiutes and other sportsmen also helped deplete the cutthroat

Since 1905 Derby Dam on the Truckee River has provided an imposing obstacle to spawning fish. Photo:Richard Dickerson.

population. During the winter and spring of 1888-89 alone, one hundred tons of Pyramid trout were shipped by Wells Fargo and by rail to points east and west and beyond.

Derby Dam on the Truckee

Dams were built across the Truckee River as early as the 1870's, but these relatively small structures didn't seriously effect Pyramid's migrating or spawning cutthroat. In 1905, however, approximately 30 miles upstream from Pyramid Lake, Derby Dam was completed by the Army Corps of Engineers. Part of the Newlands Project, this was the first federal reclamation project of its type in the country. Derby Dam fed water to a 20 mile canal in an attempt to bring electrical power and irrigation water to the Fallon area in Churchill County, Nevada. Out of token concern for the migrating and spawning cutthroat, the Corps included a temporary wooden fish ladder on one side of the dam. The ladder did not, and has never, functioned properly.

Despite the insurmountable obstacle of Derby Dam and numerous, smaller diversion dams, Pyramid's cutthroat still spawned successfully in the lower 30 miles or so of the Truckee River well into the 1920's.

During the 1920's, however, Nevada began experiencing drier-than-average winters which, coupled with water diversions at Derby Dam, caused the level of Pyramid Lake to drop steadily. With each dry year, the cutthroat found it increasingly difficult to enter the Truckee River. By 1930 the mouth of the river was choked with silt and fish could no

longer enter the river at all. Little or no spawning occurred in the Truckee during the late 1920's and early 30's as the lake's remaining trout grew to maturity.

With no small fish (from natural spawning) to confuse the issue and with the remaining cutthroat growing to giant proportions, Pyramid Lake, in the 1920's and 30's, became one of the most famous fisheries in the country. In 1925, a Paiute named John Skimmerhorn landed a 41 pound cutthroat which the International Game Fish Association (IGFA) still lists as the all-time record for cutthroat trout. People traveled from all over the country to catch trout as huge as Mr. Skimmerhorn's. Many famous people, such as Herbert Hoover and Clark Gable, fished the lake in the 1920's and 30's, adding to its allure. In fact, during this time, most people believed Pyramid was in better shape than ever.

In the late 1930's, the absence of small fish in Pyramid finally received the attention of the more observant. No juvenile fish, they reasoned, meant spawning had been interrupted. Unfortunately, these observations came too late, and, by 1940, the giant Lahontan Cutthroat of Pyramid Lake were gone.

The Original 39

Walker Lake, Nevada, like Pyramid, is believed to be a remnant of the original region-wide Lake Lahontan. Walker also supported a strain of trout classified as Oncorhynchus, Salmo Clarki Henshawi (Lahontan Cutthroat). In 1949, a commercial carp fisherman found several of the large trout in his seine. Additional seining by state fisheries person-

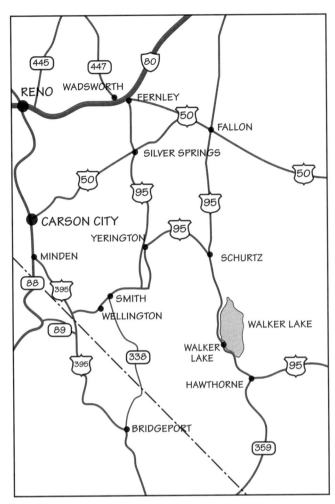

Walker Lake, one of the remnants from the original Lake Lahontan is believed to have harbored the original Pyramid Lahontan Cutthroat trout.

Why Aren't They As Big Anymore?

Overharvesting of large fish by increasing numbers of anglers combined with artificial spawning of small fish (rather than larger breeders) has had an adverse effect on the size of fish caught today. The higher salinity of the lake water and the resulting shorter life span, however, has most seriously impacted the growth rate of Pyramid's cutthroat population. In their book, *Fishes of The Great Basin: A Natural History*, Sigler and Sigler claim the Pyramid cutthroat of today live an average of six to seven years—compared to eight to nine years before the 1940's—with only a few living longer. Their study of 676 Pyramid cutthroat found average lengths of 9.1, 12.3, 15.2, 18.2, 20.6, 23.7, 25.5 inches for fish aged 1 to 7 years respectively. This is a far cry from the 30 inch plus fish commonly found before the 1940's.

Sigler and Sigler's studies also revealed "evidence the Pyramid Lake female Lahontan are alternate year spawners. This means many of them will spawn no more than twice," a theory supported by Ira LaRivers. Armed with this information, it may be possible to use the few third-time spawning females to produce a longer living strain. It very well may be a combination of these two factors—interruption of reproduction and shortened life span caused by increased salinity—which is causing the decreased size and weight of today's Lahontan Cutthroat. Hopefully, using third-time female spawners combined with normal or above-normal snow pack in the Sierra (resulting in adequate runoff) will produce larger fish.

Catch and Release

Improved spawning techniques and abundant snow pack notwithstanding, it is the angler's responsibility to help this fishery. To kill a large fish, in this day and age of catch and release, is largely an ego driven urge that should be discouraged. I have taken about 6 fish in over 28 years of fishing Pyramid Lake. I admit they are very tasty. Nevertheless, anglers today should release the majority of the fish they catch. If you must take a fish make sure it is within slot and creel regulations. Most importantly, never kill a large fish. It most likely is carrying the best genetic hope of restoring the giant Lahontan Cutthroat of the past.

If you are lucky enough to hook and land a really big cutthroat at Pyramid, be responsible. Take a picture which, with a couple of length and girth measurements, will be enough to create a plastic trophy mount. Not only will this be as attractive as a "skin" mount, it will also last longer.

nel provided a total of 39 Walker cutthroats. These were transported to the State of Nevada, Verdi Fish Hatchery where, according to Wheeler, their progeny furnished part of the spawn required to restock Pyramid and Walker Lakes.

Other lakes (e.g., Heenan Lake in Alpine County, CA and Independence Lake in Nevada and Sierra counties) also received stockings of the original Pyramid Lake Cutthroat, but it was Summit Lake (northern Humboldt County, Nevada) that provided the actual source for the reintroduction of pure-strain Lahontan cutthroat into Pyramid Lake.

Around the turn of the century, the Summit Lake Indian Reservation was established. Somewhat vague records kept at the reservation indicate there were releases of Pyramid Lake strain cutthroat into Summit Lake in the 1920's. The offspring of these Summit Lake fish were eventually "returned home" to Pyramid Lake in the mid-1970's. In the early 1980's, according to Paul Wagner, former Director of Pyramid Lake Fisheries, extensive genetic studies confirmed that these "repatriated" trout were, indeed, true Lahontan Cutthroat.

Rearing Pyramid's Cutthroat

Sutcliffe Hatchery personnel separate fish. The hatchery puts millions of small trout and about 40,000 larger fish into Pyramid Lake each year.
Photo: Reno Fly Shop.

Until 1974, the Nevada Department of Wildlife stocked Pyramid with pure-strain Lahontan and hybrid "cuttbow" trout. These fish, a cross between a cutthroat and a rainbow, adapted well to Pyramid's saline waters and grew rapidly. In 5 to 6 years they became 6 to 8 pound, hard fighting game fish. While many Pyramid anglers enjoyed catching these fast growing cuttbows, the members of the Pyramid Lake Paiute Tribe were not in favor of an "exotic" species in their lake. Consequently, with the aid of the U.S. Fish and Wildlife Service, the Paiute people began a hatchery project in 1974. The primary goal was to re-establish the native Lahontan Cutthroat in Pyramid Lake and, if possible, to restart the natural spawning run up the Truckee River. In 1976, the Paiute Tribe built its first ever "lake-water" rearing pond at the Sutcliffe Hatchery. Key to the program was an 18 inch pipe which extended far into the lake to draw lake water from a depth of 80 feet. This pond allowed hatchery fish to become acclimated to the natural water of the lake before being released. Since 1976, several more rearing ponds have been built with extra pipes and pumps added to protect the hatchery fish in the event of mechanical failure. As a result of these lake-water rearing ponds, fisheries personnel have noticed a tremendous improvement in the survival rate of newly planted trout. In 1998, the goal of the hatchery program was to plant approximately one million 8 to 10 inch trout per year. In 1997, the stocking included 40,000 fish in the 12 to 14 inch size.

Hatchery operations also include the restoration of riparian habitat along the lower Truckee River. To curtail erosion, native vegetation has been reintroduced along the river banks. To help control cattle damage of the banks, fences running 12 miles up river from the mouth were built in 1990. In addition, there is currently an ongoing effort to control the non-native beaver population. These admittedly cute but destructive creatures cause extensive damage along the riverway of the lower Truckee. The

Many cutthroat grow up in outdoor Sutcliffe Hatchery "ponds". Pure lake water is pumped up from the depths of Pyramid. *Photo: Reno Fly Shop.*

An artificial stream or raceway allows fish to spawn in the hatchery system. *Photo: Reno Fly Shop.*

success of projects like these and near-normal precipitation and runoff (which assure adequate river flow), could help re-establish a natural spawning run of Lahontan Cutthroat and Cui-ui suckers in the Truckee.

In 1997 everyone interested in this effort was encouraged when Mark Warren, a Nevada Division of Wildlife biologist, discovered a fingerling cutthroat about 10 miles up river from Pyramid. This was the first time, in recent history, that a naturally spawned Lahontan cutthroat has been found in the Truckee River below Derby Dam.

These laudable efforts by the Pyramid Lake Paiute Tribe and Pyramid Lake Fisheries, nevertheless, need to be underpinned by something as simple yet elusive as luck. From 1987 to 1994, the West suffered a major drought. Flows in the Truckee River slowed to a mere trickle during the late summer and early fall, and the water level of Pyramid Lake fell dramatically. These reduced flows deprived the lake of essential nutrients normally carried in by the river. These nutrients are vitally important and maintain the healthy food chain in the lake. Algae, zooplankton, and forage fish were greatly impacted, an impact ultimately manifested in the growth rate of Pyramid's cutthroat. During these drought years, anglers became concerned as the average size of fish caught as well as the number of large fish caught decreased.

Happily, beginning with the winter of 1994-95, the northern Sierra and the Truckee River watershed broke out of the drought and, at this time (1998), continue to enjoy above average precipitation. This change brought an immediate improvement to Pyramid Lake. The annual mean surface elevation is rising, as reported by Nancy Vucinich, the acting Resource Manager of Pyramid Lake Fisheries. In 1997 the elevation of the lake rose to 3,815 feet above sea level, the highest it has been since

1986. The '86 level was its highest level since the 1940's. As a result of this tremendous inflow, Pyramid Lake's food chain is now in excellent shape. Fisheries personnel are predicting larger and faster growing fish as well as a much improved catch rate. This rate has already jumped from 3 hours per fish in 1994-95, to 1.3 hours per fish in 1996-97.

It's obvious that the overall health of Pyramid Lake, as well as the return of cutthroat and Cui-cui to the Truckee River, depends a great deal on adequate river flow. Some guaranteed flows have been established through legislation. These mandated rates alone, unfortunately, are not enough to sustain the lake or either species' spawning runs during drought years. Only normal to above-normal snowpack in the Sierra, together with more negotiated water agreements ,will insure a healthy lake and allow the cutthroat and Cui-ui the opportunity to return to their native spawning water. As former Pyramid Fisheries Director Paul Wagner once observed, every water year is different, especially in a desert. Guaranteeing predictions about the future of the fishery is foolish. But, with the continued efforts of the Pyramid Lake tribe, the hatchery, and a little luck from Mother Nature, Pyramid Lake should remain in prime shape well into the foreseeable future.

So, despite rumors to the contrary, Oncorhynchus (Salmo) Clarki Henshawi, the Lahontan Cutthroat of Pyramid Lake, are alive and well. While the original trout of Pyramid Lake are considered extinct by some, the strain in the lake today is assuredly a true Lahontan Cutthroat, appearing in all respects to be of the original strain. With proper management and more wet years in the Sierra Nevada, these trout have the potential to grow to the tremendous size they were at the turn of the century.

A Lahontan Cutthroat feeding on Tui Chub.

Food and Feeding Habits of Pyramid Cutthroat Trout

Despite its rather barren appearance, Pyramid Lake is a veritable smorgasbord of trout food: from plankton to the endangered cui-ui (pronounced kwee-wee), a lake sucker held sacred by the Paiute Tribe. Understanding this food chain will help anglers of all kinds. This background also enhances anyone's appreciation of this high desert lake.

Wydoski and Whitney in *Inland Fishes of Washington* found that "a majority of inland subspecies of cutthroat trout feed primarily on aquatic insects, while larger fish may feed entirely on other fish." On the other hand, La Rivers in *Fishes and Fisheries of Nevada* and Sigler and Sigler in *Fishes of the Great Basin* state that Pyramid Lake cutthroat as small as 13 inches begin feeding on smaller

fish such as the tui chub (pronounced two-ee). As these fish mature, the importance of fish in their diet increases dramatically. According to Sigler and Sigler, "the diet of fish that are 20 to 30 inches long is about 94% fish and almost entirely tui chub." Large cutthroat have even been known to contain smaller cutthroat in their stomachs after they were caught and examined.

While other fish are an important part of the cutthroat's diet, determined Pyramid anglers should know about the variety other foods available to these fish. The following list is from La Rivers *Fishes and Fisheries of Nevada* and from my personal observations. As this is a "no-nonsense" guidebook, this list is general, but it will give anglers an idea of why Pyramid cutthroat take a variety of flies.

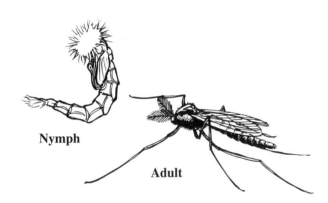

1) **Midge**, Order Diptera. In the fall, smaller cutthroat sip midges in less than 1 foot of water.

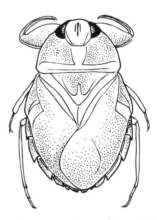

3) **Crawling Water Bug**, Order Hemiptera. Small water bugs, a possible reason small #8-10 flies are successful at Pyramid.

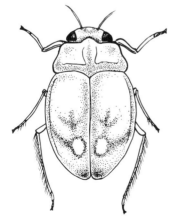

2) **Beetle**, Order Coleoptera. Including predaceous water beetles, herbivorous water beetles, crawling water beetles, mud beetles.

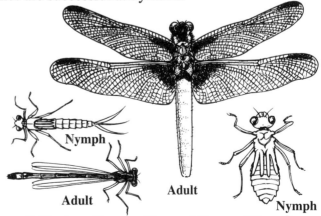

4) **Various Dragonflies and Damselflies**, Order Odonata. These probably explain the success of Woolly Worms, Buggers and similar patterns.

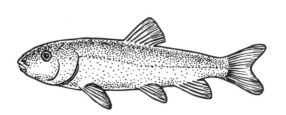

5) Scuds, Order Crustacea. Gammarus scuds are found in rocky areas of the lake. As tiny as size #20, they are not an important food for large cutthroat.

8) Lake Suckers or Cui-ui. A possible food for Pyramid's large cutthroat. The spawning male's back is black or brown with red to brassy colors on the sides, which fade to a flat white on the belly. The female has a bluish-gray cast. Once thought a bottom feeder in the vast depths, studies show cui-ui feed in water 30 to 100 feet. Here they feed on small invertebrates, some aquatic insects, and occasionally algae. Cui-ui can live 18 years or more, and grow to 27 inches and 6 pounds. The practical fly pattern size is 2 to 5 inches long.

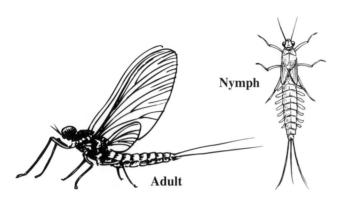

Nymph

Adult

6) Mayflies, Order Ephemeroptera. From late March-May, small fish feed fairly regularly on Callibaetis - mottle-winged, gray mayflies, #14-18. Rarely have large cutthroat been observed taking these insects on the surface.

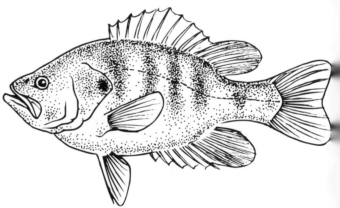

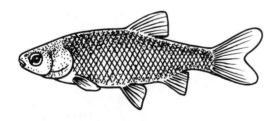

7) Tui Chub, Approximately 90% of a large Pyramid cutthroat's diet consists of bait fish, and the tui chub is the mainstay. Tui chub are deep olive colored along their back, lighter olive on their sides, and white with a hint of yellow on their bellies. Backs and sides often give off a brassy reflection. Fins are olive, tinted with red. Tui chub can live up to 7 years, attaining a size of 16 inches. The most common size eaten by large fish is 3 to 5 inches.

9) Sacramento Perch, were introduced from California's Central Valley in the 1880's. A deep bodied fish with a greenish-purple, metallic sheen, the perch's back is bluish-white to brown. Black mottles on the sides change to white and silver on the belly. There are 6 or 7 dark, irregular vertical bars on the sides and a large blackish dot on the gill covers.

These fish have inhabited Pyramid Lake for over 100 years but don't flourish. Late spring to early fall, fish for them near structure and rocky outcroppings. Caught at Pyramid Lake, the all-tackle record for the Sacramento perch weighed 4 lbs. 9 ounces. Larger fish have been reported in other waters. It is believed that, under proper conditions, these fish can reach a weight of 10 pounds.

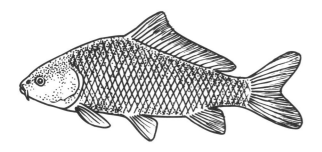

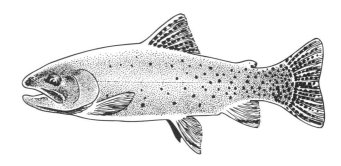

10) Asiatic carp. Also introduced into the lake in the 1880's, these carp inhabit the southern end of Pyramid where flows from the Truckee River help maintain a fair population. These carp are medium olive on their back which fades to a yellowish-gold on their sides. Their bottom fins sometimes have a rosy tinge. Pyramid specimens have grown in excess of 3 feet in length.

11) Lahontan Cutthroat, are aggressive feeders that consume just about anything smaller than themselves. With large fish feeding mainly on smaller fish, it seems a mystery they even bother to take aquatic bugs. This is possibly due to a conditioned response imprinted during the first few years of their life when they fed exclusively on small insects. With the array of food available to Pyramid's cutthroat, it's easy to understand why they will take a number of different fly imitations.

The cutthroat must be feeding on a lot of tui chub as evidenced by this line of fly fishers. This is a busy day at the "North Nets" near the Sutcliffe Hatchery.   *Photo: Reno Fly Shop.*

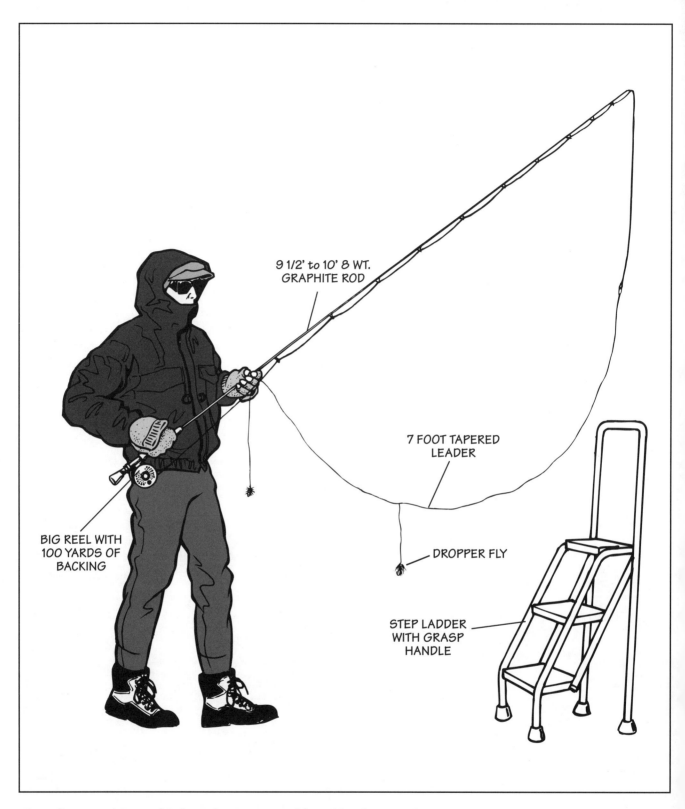

9 1/2' to 10' 8 WT. GRAPHITE ROD

7 FOOT TAPERED LEADER

DROPPER FLY

STEP LADDER WITH GRASP HANDLE

BIG REEL WITH 100 YARDS OF BACKING

The well-equipped Pyramid Lake angler. Be prepared for cold and wet weather. Dress in layers and bring your big fly rod!

Tackle & Equipment for Pyramid Lake

Not for the weak of heart or rod

*F*rom heavy tippets and stripping baskets to step ladders, there's not much about the gear needed to properly fly fish Pyramid Lake that suggests the genteel, "fine and far off" activity of traditional fresh water fly fishing. The tackle most commonly used to fish Pyramid is more frequently associated with steelhead or surf fishing than with trout fishing on inland still water. Long, relatively heavy, graphite rods used to chunk 30 foot shooting heads backed with a 100 feet of running or shooting line are often the norm. Luckily, the list of tackle and equipment needed to fish Pyramid is short and basic, but anglers should not look in their traditional trout gear to fill the list. This is the "X-Games" of fly fishing; it's not for the weak of heart or rod.

Rods

Because strong winds are known to come up suddenly at Pyramid, lighter rods are not commonly used. Nine to 9 1/2, or even 10 foot graphite rods capable of throwing 8 or 9 weight shooting heads are recommended. These longer rods allow the caster to keep his or her back cast higher. Not slapping the water on the back cast helps lengthen the forward cast. A 9 1/2 foot, 7 weight graphite rod works best for me.

Reels

Saltwater reels are ideal for Pyramid due to the salinity of the lake water. Like me, however, I suspect most anglers do not have the money to sink into a nice saltwater reel. Happily, freshwater reels work just fine if they are flushed with warm, fresh water after each outing. A good Pyramid reel should also have the capacity to hold the appropriate sized shooting head and running line plus at least 100 yards of 20 pound backing. Pyramid trout are not "reel burners." Their run is more like a bulldog than a bonefish. There is, however, always the chance of hooking the big trout of a lifetime. Because of their size and strength, some of the larger fish hooked at Pyramid can take an angler well into his or her backing. It's best to be prepared.

Lines

From different types of full-length fly lines to shooting tapers, the lines recommended by Pyramid anglers seem as varied as these individuals.

At one time or another all have been effective. In early fall and again in spring as the lake's cutthroat move in closer to shore, for example, intermediate or even floating lines will sometimes work.

All fishing is a function of time spent in the water, and this is especially true in trying to hook a good fish at Pyramid. Chances are, the harder you work at casting, the less time you'll stay out. For repetitive distance casting, no line is more "user friendly" than a shooting taper.

Shooting Heads

The most proven technique for hooking Lahontan Cutthroat is to fish the fly right on the bottom. For this important reason and ease of casting, I find that a super-fast sinking shooting taper or "head" backed by a 100 feet or so of good running line works best. Thirty-foot shooting heads or tapers, as opposed to full 80 or 90 foot fly lines, are recommended for one reason — casting distance. From 6 to 14 weight, from floating to super-fast sink, there are many different types of shooting tapers on the market today. Most rod manufactures recommend using a shooting head one weight heavier than the rod calls for. A 7 weight rod requires an 8 weight shooting head to achieve maximum performance; an 8 weight rod will require a 9 weight head, etc..

While manufacturers market shooting tapers as light as 6 weight, I do not advise using them to fish Pyramid. Even a slight breeze can adversely effect casting distance, especially when using a light line. Conversely, heavier lines in the 10 or larger weights can unnecessarily tire an angler after only a short time. As mentioned above, my preferred line is an 8 weight, super-fast sinking, shooting head. This 8 weight "head" is heavy enough to punch through fairly strong winds, and I can cast it for long periods of time without undue fatigue.

Shooting or Running Lines

As with "heads," there are several varieties of running lines from which to chose, including monofilament, braided, and floating. Regardless of their other attributes, all running lines need to be stretched before casting.

Monofilament running lines such as Amnesia and Cobra are available in 15 to 30 pound strength

No Nonsense Double-Haul

①After completing the forward cast, the angler gives a sharp pull with the line hand immediately after beginning the backcast.

②After completing the backcast, the angler gives another sharp pull with his line hand immediately after beginning the forward cast.

For water the size of Pyramid Lake, the added distance gained by using the "double-haul" can be very useful. The casting stroke itself is normal... but the action of the line hand shown in the illustrations will add a good deal of line speed and consequently, distance to your casts.

③ Now the final forward cast is made and the line is shot out through the guides.

Shooting or Running Lines - continued

with 20 or 25 pound the most commonly used. With its thin diameter and smooth surface, a properly stretched and dressed monofilament running line will, theoretically, cast further than other running lines. However, its primary drawback — a tendency to tightly coil in cold water — tends to negate this advantage in casting distance, especially in the 40 or so degree water often encountered at Pyramid.

Braided running lines, while still needing to be dressed to keep them afloat, require little stretching. Most will not coil as bad as monofilament running lines when fished in cold water.

Floating running lines work best under all conditions at Pyramid Lake. They float better and have less "memory" in cold water. Their only drawback is the loss of a few feet in casting distance due to their larger diameters. After three decades of fishing Pyramid I've found that a cast that's a few feet short makes no difference in the number of hook-ups. Furthermore, properly dressed, floating running lines are subject to less water drag and resist coiling in 40 degree water — two positive factors in distance casting that far outweigh the negative of their larger diameters. Additionally, when well cared for, they will provide 2 to 3 years of dependable service, even with lots of use.

As mentioned earlier, other types of lines are used at Pyramid, but all present problems. Weight forward, sink-tip lines, for example, will not allow a beginning, intermediate, and even some expert casters the distance necessary to effectively fish the lake. Full, 90 foot sinking lines are not recommended for the same reason. Anglers who have no other line or simply prefer to use a sink-tip or full sinking line should choose one with a sink rate of III or IV to allow the fly to sink as fast as possible.

One final note on "double hauling". If shooting heads are the preferred lines for fishing Pyramid, then the double haul cast is the preferred technique. Simply stated, anglers who have taken the time to learn and practice their double haul will be more successful than those who don't. Again, Pyramid is a distance casters lake: the more water the fly covers, the better chance of hooking up.

The illustrations at left are a good introduction to the double haul, but just an introduction. Ask any accomplished fly angler and they'll tell you the only way to learn the double haul cast is to try it and practice it. It's the fly casting equivalent to simultaneously rubbing your stomach and patting your head. Try it on a pond, or better yet, take a lesson.

Leaders

Pyramid cutthroat are not very leader shy, and they have numerous large teeth and hard mouths.

Heavier tippets allow anglers to set the hook hard and fast; light tippets will simply not take the abuse of heavy fly tackle fighting a 10 pound fish. 6 to 7 1/2 foot leaders tapering to 8 to 10 pounds test work best. These shorter leaders will get a fly to the bottom faster and will have less stretch when setting the hook.

A lot of anglers like to fish Pyramid with two flies. About 12 to 14 inches from the tip of the leader, they attach an 8 inch dropper, usually about 1X stronger than the tippet (see knots). To present a range of color to the fish, they most often tie a dark fly on the point or end of the leader and a light or bright fly on the dropper (or vice-versa). These two-fly combinations work very well either way. The only drawback is an occasional double hook-up.

Waders and Layered Clothing

It can get cold at Pyramid and here's proof. A friend once got out of the water to answer a call of nature. Pyramid's 39 degree water left him numb from the waist down. He reached into his waders and pulled out his shirt tail. Being too cold in all extremities to realize his mistake, he then proceeded to take a leak inside his waders.

Layering seems to be the catch word for any outdoor activity. Casting a shooting head at Pyramid is no different, especially during the more productive months of November through April. Even on a beautiful day in October or April, however, a well prepared angler always brings enough clothing to layer his or her body. Pyramid's frequent storms are usually accompanied by high winds and snow. A warm fall or spring day can quickly turn cold, wet and miserable.

The properly dressed Pyramid Lake angler, Jose Silva layered his clothing and is ready for the worst cold, wind, snow and rain the west can dish out. This is not the person mentioned in the story above. Photo: Reno Fly Shop.

❖ 14 ❖

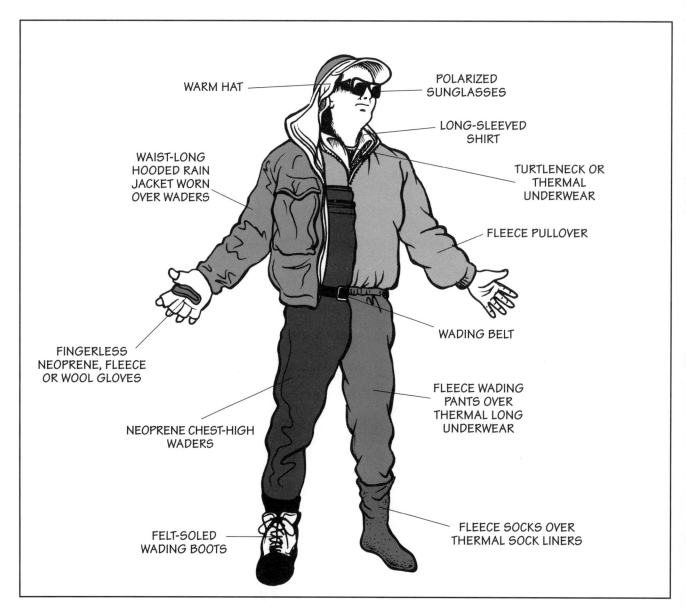

WARM HAT

POLARIZED SUNGLASSES

LONG-SLEEVED SHIRT

WAIST-LONG HOODED RAIN JACKET WORN OVER WADERS

TURTLENECK OR THERMAL UNDERWEAR

FLEECE PULLOVER

WADING BELT

FINGERLESS NEOPRENE, FLEECE OR WOOL GLOVES

FLEECE WADING PANTS OVER THERMAL LONG UNDERWEAR

NEOPRENE CHEST-HIGH WADERS

FELT-SOLED WADING BOOTS

FLEECE SOCKS OVER THERMAL SOCK LINERS

Comfort when fishing in Pyramid Lake weather means staying warm and dry. Body heat must stay in. Moisture must wick away. Cold, wet and wind must stay out. Fortunately there is enough lightweight, waterproof, "breathable" and windproof outdoor clothing available today to keep just about everyone happy. The key is to wear several layers. This way you can always take off or put on to adjust to conditions. Whenever you're going to Pyramid take the essentials listed above.

Suffice it to say, to comfortably fish Pyramid, quality chest high neoprene waders worn over a "wicking" layer of the best long underwear bottoms and socks are a must. Try a good polypropylene top and a warm long sleeve shirt, followed by some type of fleece insulating layer such as a jacket or pullover. A good, waist-long, hooded rain jacket not tucked in but worn outside of the waders will keep rolling waves from splashing water over waders. This water, as we all know, will inevitably trickle down and collect in the foot area. For anglers who wade deep, these jackets also keep elbows dry. The hood not only helps keep the head warm, but on windy days, protects it from being whacked by a large, wildly off-course fly. On really cold days, I also like to wear a knit cap which fits comfortably

under my rain jacket hood. Finally, and especially on the coldest days, a good pair of fingerless neoprene, fleece, or wool gloves are mighty welcome when a brisk, cold wind starts to blow over wet hands.

Float Tubes and Prams

This story explains my opinion of using these craft on Pyramid. Once an absent minded float tubing friend of mine lost track of how far he had drifted from Pyramid's western shore. He also didn't pay attention to what sailors call a freshening breeze. This breeze ultimately "freshened" into a full-blown wind storm. By the time he noticed his predicament, it was too late, too late even for a rescue effort that had to be called off due to high winds and "seas."

It's best __not__ to use a float tube or pram to fly fish Pyramid. Every now and then there is a clear, perfectly still day when a tube is safe. Nevada angler Richard Dickerson is shown on one of those days.   Photo: David Banks.

For several hours, into the frigid night, he was blown across the lake until his tube finally came to rest on Anejo Island. There, until he was rescued the next day, he spent the remainder of what had to be the coldest, most miserable, and probably luckiest night of his life. Despite stories like these, the use of float tubes and prams has become increasingly popular at Pyramid Lake. I don't advocate their use for two reasons: they're difficult to fish out of and, since not everyone is as fortunate as my friend, they can be dangerous.

Float tubes in Pyramid are more trouble than they are worth. In a tube, the angler is at the mercy of the wind and constantly kicking either toward or away from shore. In addition, it's much harder to cast and fish from a tube. Effective distance casting with a shooting head is difficult enough with both feet planted, let alone with wind blowing the angler in every direction. If you must fish from a tube, I suggest using a sink-tip or full sinking line. Either of these are easier to control from a tube than a shooting taper system. The wind blown, float tube angler also has difficulty controlling line while fishing, making it hard to detect strikes and play fish. Even 20 inch Pyramid cutthroat will fight for a long time. I've watched more tubers than I care to count play fish to near exhaustion mainly because without firm footing, they had no way to land them. When fishing Pyramid from a float tube, responsible and careful anglers use a good sized net to minimize stressing the fish. They also use some kind of anchor to hedge against potent Pyramid winds.

It's also foolhardy to use a small pram to fish Pyramid. The lake can go from dead calm to rolling white caps in a matter of minutes. Waves have swamped boats up to 18 feet long. What chance does an angler in an 8 or 10 foot fly fishing pram have in similar conditions? Unfortunately, someone drowns at Pyramid almost every year. Most of these drowning victims were in small, overloaded boats that were too far from shore when heavy winds came up.

Pram anglers who still wish to brave Pyramid's unpredictable weather should at least improve their odds. Always check the weather report before venturing out. If you can't obtain a weather report, check at the ranger station or one of the stores near the lake.

There's an old saying at Pyramid: "Dust clouds at the North end of the lake mean 15 minutes to get off the water." A float tube or a pram angler who sees these dust clouds or a dark line of advancing waves should immediately move close to shore, so they can quickly get out of the water. Better yet, wade the shoreline. It's an easier and more effective way to fish Pyramid, not to mention much, much safer.

Step Ladders and Milk Crates

Why get elevated? Because elevated anglers can fish deeper, and it's easier to cast. The use of milk crates and step ladders as casting platforms has been going on for as long as anglers have fly fished Pyramid from shore. During the early years, the milk crate seemed to work best. It was easy to transport, easy to sink in the water, and provided a fairly stable, if small, platform from which to cast. In the 1970's, however, milk crates gradually gave way to small, 3 or 4 rung, step ladders. Finally, in the mid '80's, ladders took over as the technology of choice for discriminating Pyramid anglers, prompted, I suspect, by the $50 fine the local dairy charged its customers for missing milk crates.

Either platform - milk crate or step ladder - helps elevate an angler, allowing a farther wade out to deeper water. If the "surf" is rolling in, one can stay closer to shore and remain above these rolling waves. As with any fishing, the longer the fly is in the water, the better chance for a hook up. Walking a milk crate or step ladder out as far as possible allows an angler to reach water not available to the regular wader. Sometimes this distance makes the critical difference between fish and no fish. The additional height also helps keep an angler's back cast above the water, and a good back cast is 90% of a good distance cast.

Many anglers "mark" their platform, using some type of buoy on a rope 5-10 feet long or enough to reach the surface from the bottom. Nothing (short of falling in) can ruin a day at Pyramid like having to reach down into the water to right a crate or ladder that has fallen over while unattended. Duck decoys make an excellent buoy, but anything that floats will work.

This laid back Pyramid fly rodder uses the grasp handle on the step ladder for support. He has walked the ladder as far out into the lake as possible to fish hard-to-reach water.
Photo: Terry Barron

The downside of using a milk crate or step ladder as a casting platform is that they both limit movement. They are cumbersome to move even short distances and make the angler more visible to the fish. As trout go, Lahontan Cutthroat are not considered very smart. Still, they do have a well-honed instinct for the predator/prey relationship. It should

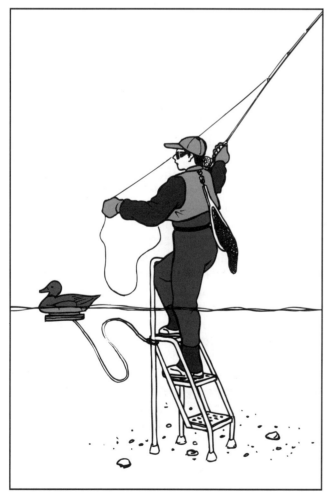

Some anglers use a duck decoy or plastic jug to help locate their ladder if it falls over.

be presumed that the easier it is for them to see the angler the less likely they will be to take his or her fly. For these reasons, an increasing number of Pyramid anglers simply wade-fish the lake.

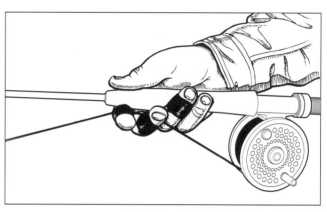

Wrap electrical tape around the fingers of the rod hand to prevent burns or cuts caused by line that runs through fingers while you strip line back in.

Stripping or Shooting Baskets

These devices seem to be either loved or hated. Because they keep my running line from sinking or being pushed by the wind, I enjoy using them. Pyramid means distance casting, and by holding the running line out of the water, a shooting basket eliminates the distance killing factor of water drag. Some distance casters, in an attempt to reduce drag, try to hold their running lines in their mouths or hands, but I have never been able to grasp the effectiveness of this technique. Shooting baskets also make it convenient to move short distances. Just strip your line into the basket and you can easily move several feet left or right and quickly resume casting.

The one great disadvantage of a stripping basket is that, unless used while on top a milk crate or step ladder, it limits how deep you can wade. The bottom of the basket must be kept out of the water so the running line won't tangle. Since the basket is worn around the lower chest or waist, you are restricted to wading shallow water. There are shooting baskets on the market with egg carton-like bumps on the bottom. These allow a small bit of water in the basket while keeping a shooting line from tangling. I've not tried one, but anglers who have say they work fine.

The fly fishing tackle and equipment— especially rods, reels and lines— listed here are the most commonly used and effective at Pyramid Lake. If you have a 5 or 10 weight rod, or any other gear that does not exactly match what I recommend, don't be discouraged from fishing the lake. As with any type of fishing, it's the angler's skill and the amount of time on the water, rather than equipment, that are the most important factors in hooking the big one at Pyramid.

A stripping basket, worn around the waist, helps one manage all that line that one casts and then pulls or strips back. Some think they are essential, some don't. The author does.
Photo: David Banks

Area angler Ron Privrasky shows what it's like when it all comes together at Pyramid Lake. *Photo: Ann Privrasky.*

Ann Privrasky with a beautiful cutthroat caught by her husband, Ron.
Photo: Ron Privrasky.

When & Where to Fly Fish Pyramid Lake

Pyramid Lake Fly Fishing Conditions By The Month

*U*se these generalizations to help plan your Pyramid Lake fly fishing outing. These are based on the past 30 years of fishing. Water conditions can vary from year to year as can seasons and regulations which can affect these conditions. Always consult a fly shop, or the resources in the back of this guidebook to get the latest information.

JAN	FEB	MAR	APR	MAY	JUN	JUL	AUG	SEP	OCT	NOV	DEC
Fair to Good Depends on Weather	Fair to Good Depends on Weather	Good Depends on Weather	Prime	Good	Good	Closed	Closed	Closed	Prime to Good Opens October First	Prime	Prime first two weeks Depends on Weather

The lake water cools October through May. Pyramid's cutthroat also spawn at this time. They move close to shore and following its contours, seek freshwater inlets in which to lay eggs. During these months, when the spawning urge combines with the Lahontan Cutthroat's natural curiosity and aggressiveness, fly fishing is prime. The wading fly angler has the best opportunity to experience great still water fishing with the chance of hooking the trout of a lifetime.

The erratic nature of the Lahontan Cutthroat, and Pyramid Lake, make it difficult to specify exact times of day or year that insure fishing success. For example, while Pyramid's cutthroat have been observed feeding on the surface every month of the year, hatches are unpredictable, unlike most other high desert lakes. Dry fly fishing at the lake is chancy at best. Still, experienced Pyramid anglers all have their favorite times to be in the water. Here is my rule of thumb:

You can catch fish from early fall through late spring. November to early December and March to May are generally Pyramid's most productive months. This is when water temperatures range from 50-55 degrees, considered best for cutthroat.

Water temperature must always be considered when choosing the time of day and time of year to fish Pyramid. Some anglers prefer mornings while others only fish the last hours of daylight. Like many other veteran Pyramid anglers, I prefer morning fishing in the early fall and again from late winter through spring. In the dead of winter, when water temperatures are in the low 40's, evenings are my favorite time. Generally, low-light periods of the day

or a dark, overcast sky produce the best action. Stormy weather almost always produces some of the hottest fishing at Pyramid. Given the opportunity, I make a point of fishing during an incoming storm front, regardless of the time of day.

Where to Fish

Most anglers will be intimidated by the size of the lake, especially fishing Pyramid for the first time. Not surprisingly, one of the most frequent questions is "Where is the best spot to fish?" I can't seem to think of any bad spots. Fact is, there are few places around the lake where a persistent angler won't catch fish.

On the following maps, I have marked some of Pyramid's most popular fishing spots. These places all have fish, but, at times, some have more than others. One of the best ways to figure out where to fish is to look for other anglers. It's surprising the speed "word of mouth" travels when the subject is a hot fishing spot at Pyramid. A long line of anglers standing out in the water is a sure bet that somebody is catching something. Just observe these other fishermen. If any of them are hooking fish, then it's probably a good idea to wade out and give the area a try.

If nobody's catching anything at the "usual spots" or if, like me, you don't care to fish in a crowd, keep driving around. Stop and fish any of the thousands of lesser known and, consequently, less frequented spots around Pyramid Lake. That's how you find new hot spots.

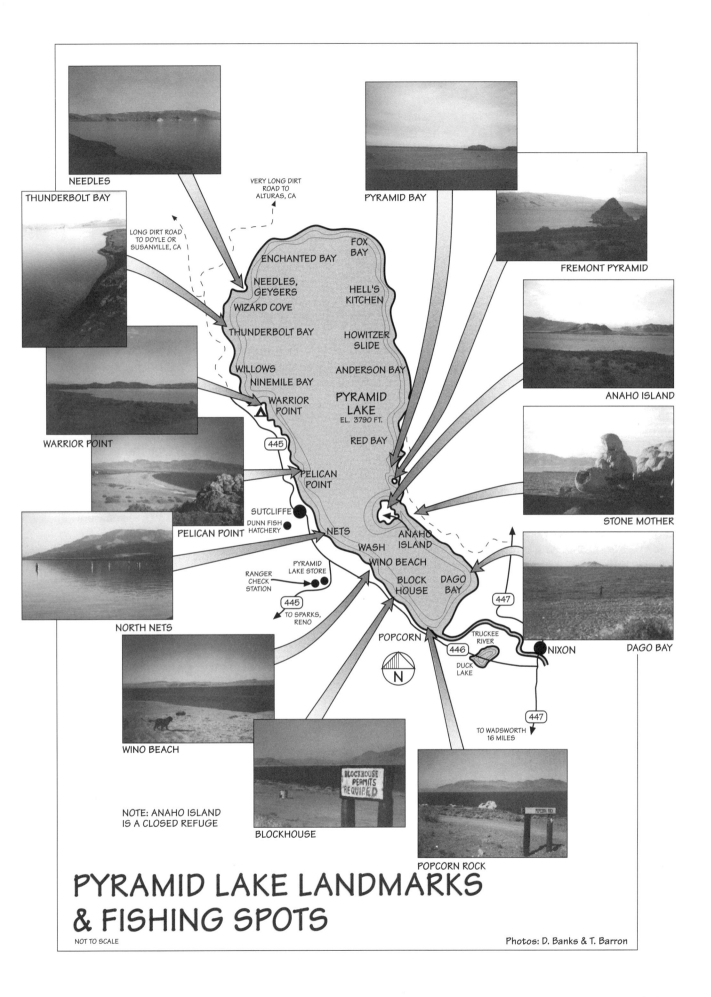

NEEDLES

THUNDERBOLT BAY

VERY LONG DIRT ROAD TO ALTURAS, CA

LONG DIRT ROAD TO DOYLE OR SUSANVILLE, CA

PYRAMID BAY

FREMONT PYRAMID

FOX BAY

ENCHANTED BAY

NEEDLES, GEYSERS

WIZARD COVE

HELL'S KITCHEN

THUNDERBOLT BAY

HOWITZER SLIDE

WILLOWS

NINEMILE BAY

ANDERSON BAY

WARRIOR POINT

PYRAMID LAKE
EL. 3790 FT.

RED BAY

ANAHO ISLAND

STONE MOTHER

WARRIOR POINT

445

PELICAN POINT

SUTCLIFFE

DUNN FISH HATCHERY

PELICAN POINT

NETS

ANAHO ISLAND

WASH

WINO BEACH

PYRAMID LAKE STORE

RANGER CHECK STATION

BLOCK HOUSE

DAGO BAY

447

445

TO SPARKS, RENO

NORTH NETS

POPCORN

TRUCKEE RIVER

NIXON

DAGO BAY

446

DUCK LAKE

N

447

TO WADSWORTH 16 MILES

WINO BEACH

NOTE: ANAHO ISLAND IS A CLOSED REFUGE

BLOCKHOUSE
PERMITS
REQUIRED

BLOCKHOUSE

POPCORN ROCK

PYRAMID LAKE LANDMARKS
& FISHING SPOTS

NOT TO SCALE

Photos: D. Banks & T. Barron

❖ 20 ❖

How to Try a New Spot

Finding and trying a new spot means getting in the water. Here's how I suggest you investigate a part of the lake you've never fished before. Start by rigging up and wading out up to your knees. Strip out the head and about 20 feet of running line. Cast around 5 to 10 times before lengthening your cast. During each cast, count to see how long it takes the fly to reach the bottom. This gives an estimation of the depth of the water. I call this "search casting".

On average, a super-fast sinking shooting head sinks about 6 inches per-second. A slow 7 count, for example, means you are fishing in about 4 feet of water. Continue with the 5 to 10 "casting sets" until you're consistently casting the shooting head as far as you can. If you don't get a strike, wade out as deep as possible and continue casting.

At the end of each cast, retrieve the fly along the bottom using short, steady, 6 to 10 inch strips. Occasionally vary the speed of the retrieve, though a short, steady strip works best most of the time. If you fail to hook anything after a couple of hours or so, move to another area either by walking or driving along the shoreline. It's not uncommon to move 3 or 4 times before finding fish.

Look for Ledges and Drops

Pyramid's cutthroat seem to prefer swimming along the ledges of the lake's relatively shallow shoreline. These ledges do not have to be high, a 6 inch ledge is enough for these fish. I look for likely ledges by feeling the bottom with my fly when I do my search casting. After finding a good ledge, I keep casting over it. Don't be in a hurry to move on. Spend enough time to allow fish to come to you. If I feel anything interrupt my retrieve, I strike hard and fast. Assume you're hooking the ledge, however, if you feel an interruption at about the same place on every retrieve. Hooking a ledge feels remarkably like a fish taking a fly. I have often struck 3 or more times before I realize that what I'm feeling is actually my fly catching the lip of one of these sand ledges. When you catch the lip of a huge cutthroat, you'll know the difference!

Pyramid cutts also like to hold or cruise near the steep drop-offs along some of the deeper sections of shoreline. I use the same technique of deep, search casting when fishing these areas. Drop-offs feel much different than ledges; usually, like a lead sinker has been added to and then suddenly taken away from the end of the line. I get an indication of the dimensions of the drop-off by how long the "added sinker" portion of my retrieve lasts.

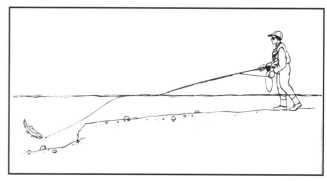

Fish the ledges and drop-offs along the shoreline, the key to finding Pyramid's cutthroat.

One of the hardest types of strikes to detect is when a fish hits while the fly is traveling up a drop-off. When fishing these areas, always strike sharply if you feel anything that seems even a little out of the ordinary.

Despite what appears to be a clean, sandy bottom, there are evil snags lurking under Pyramid's clear water. In high water years, when the lake level has risen above the sage brush, you'll find lots of snags.

Snags feel much different than ledges or drop-offs. They don't let go! If I get hung up on a snag, I try to get hold of my shooting head, not my running line, before I attempt to break the line free. Don't jerk on the snag, even if your shooting head is in the reel. Point your rod tip at the snag and back up, using small steps, until you feel the fly or leader break free. Sometimes you lose all this, but you'll help employ fly tiers like me.

The feel of ledges, drop-offs, and snags become familiar after repeated retrieves, a familiarity directly proportionate to the condition of your fly's hook. I make it a point (no pun intended) to keep my hook de-barbed and sharp. Check it frequently and re-sharpen if necessary. Even though you should be wary of getting hung up on a snag, always be prepared for a take at any time. Always strike hard and fast when you feel something even slightly different as you retrieve a fly over the bottom.

Pay Attention

As with any type of fishing, focus is an important quality to cultivate. Pyramid Lake is beautiful, at times breathtakingly so, and it's easy to start drifting, especially when fishing solo. I don't know how many times I've been shaken out of a pleasant daydream by a striking fish. This usually results in a failed hookup. To combat my tendency to skylark, I try to concentrate on keeping my rod tip just above or slightly in the water while retrieving the fly. This not only gives me something to focus on, but also allows plenty of room to bring the rod tip up hard and fast when a fish hits. A gentle set, the product

A Pyramid Lake trophy. When you lose your concentration while endlessly casting away at Pyramid Lake, stay focused by thinking about the huge fish that will strike, and the great photo you'll have to show everyone.   Photo: Reno Fly Shop

of a daydream or not, usually means a lost fish. This concentration is the same sort of focus used by devoted steelheaders to ward off inattention caused by repetitive motions and casts.

When a Pyramid cutthroat sees a fly, it will usually follow it and then strike. It's not uncommon for these fish to strike a fly more than once on a single retrieve. If you feel a hit but miss the fish, stop. Recover slack line and then hesitate for a few seconds before continuing your retrieve. I retrieve my line until I see my fly in the water. I'm in no hurry to yank it out for the next cast. Many Pyramid fish have been hooked when the fly has been no more than 10 feet from the rod tip. This is exciting.

Keep At It

Like fish everywhere, Pyramid's cutthroat are not always cooperative. Despite my best, most focused efforts, there have been days when I leave the lake feeling like I've definitely been "given the fin." These are the times when I reflect on the nature of still water fishing in general and Pyramid Lake fishing in particular.

Remember, in Pyramid the terrific cutthroat are at the top of the food chain and in *their* realm. They are governed only by the oxygen content in the water and the shoreline of the lake. Unlike stream fish, who must contend with current, still water trout are free to travel where they please.

They eat about anything they want without expending a great deal of energy. At times, trout will key on a particular hatch. Other times, they feed when the opportunity presents itself. Still other times it seems like they'll never eat again. Keep these thoughts in mind when having a tough day or you are impatient to move to another spot. When the fishing is slow, try to learn more about the particular part of the shoreline you're fishing. Move left or right, 10 to 20 feet, casting at every stop (10 to 20 times). Finally, always be grateful to be spending "another day in Paradise." It beats working!

Regardless of the time, place, or method used to fly fish Pyramid Lake, the best way to insure success is to stay in the water and cast. Keep the fly in the water as much as possible, moving it along the bottom. Out of town anglers need to stay at least a few days and fish more than 1 or 2 hours in order to experience and adjust to the many different conditions of the lake. Every day at Pyramid is different and anglers who take the time to hone their skills and learn the water will most certainly have big fish stories to tell.

Flies for Pyramid Trout

Basic Information and Favorite Patterns

*I*t's not too difficult to understand why Pyramid cutts are caught on a variety of lures and flies and at any time by shore and boat anglers. Just combine the variety of food available with their curious and aggressive behavior, and their tendency to cruise the shoreline from the fall through the spring months.

In the last 20 years, fly fishing has really become popular at Pyramid. Today there are as many fly anglers at the lake as any other type of fisher. A simple reason for this is the popularity of fly fishing in general. The fact is, a fly caster has as much chance of hooking a large Pyramid cutthroat as a troller or spin fisherman. In recent years some of the largest fish in the lake have been caught by fly anglers casting from shore. Be optimistic.

Many new fly designs are being created these days. Because presentation is usually more important than pattern at Pyramid, most of these new patterns are merely a result of the boom of colorful synthetic materials flooding the fly tying market. These new materials are largely displacing fur and hair, but happily not hackle, as mainstays of a fly tier's materials list. They are but slight variations of the basic flies that have been producing for Pyramid anglers for decades.

Try Patterns That Catch

What follows are a variety of proven Pyramid patterns. Since the cutthroat in Pyramid are notoriously opportunistic feeders, however, you shouldn't be discouraged from tying and trying your own favorite ugly bug patterns. I encourage experimentation and improvisation though some angler's feel they must precisely imitate the patterns listed in books, or they'll be unsuccessful. While this can be true, especially for those just learning to tie, it should not prevent the intermediate or advanced tier from trying other ideas. As evidenced by the following flies, everyone has a favorite pattern, and you will eventually find one too. This is important because I believe that confidence in the fly I'm fishing is my most effective fishing tool.

Woolly Power

Strange as it seems, the work horse fly for Pyramid Lake is the lowly Woolly Worm. I can almost see eyebrows raise and hear voices cry out, "Surely there must be a better fly?" Maybe there is, but I've been looking for over 28 years, and have yet to find a pattern more consistently successful than the Woolly Worm. I'm not going to argue with the angler who had a great day with another fly, it happens and will continue to happen. But as anyone who has fly fished for more than a couple of years knows, flies come and go, but there are a few patterns that can always be counted on to catch fish. For fly fishing Pyramid Lake, the Woolly Worm is one of these enduring patterns.

The well-stocked Pyramid fly box should always include a variety of light and dark patterns in several sizes. "Dark day, dark fly, bright day, bright fly" is a good rule to keep in mind when fishing Pyramid lake. If you don't tie your own flies, there are several shops listed in the back of this book that carry complete selections of Pyramid patterns. If you do tie, or would like to learn how, the next section is the inside information you've been waiting for.

Tying Flies For Pyramid

Although the Mustad 9672 is the traditional hook for the Woolly Worm and the Tiemco 200R will also work just fine, I prefer to tie my Woolly Worms on a Mustad 3906B or Tiemco (TMC) 3761 in sizes 2 through 8. The 2X shank of these hooks is long enough for the proportions of the fly, and their large hook gap helps hook Pyramid's tough-mouthed cutthroat. Also, I'm not stingy with my hackles and suggest these flies get at least two saddle hackles. Three or four are even better. Finally, I never weight my Pyramid flies. I want my fly on the bottom not *in* the bottom.

Black/Black/Red
Woolly Worm

Rainbow/Black
Woolly Worm

Black/Pearl Wing
Woolly Worm

Chartreuse/White
Woolly Worm

White Estaz/White
Woolly Worm

Purple/Pearl Wing
Woolly Worm

Dave Stanley's
Dragon Nymph

Pink/White
Woolly Worm

Mark Tilton's
Tui Chub Streamer

Ike Berry's
Foam Beetle

Glen Allred's
Hard Body Sculpin

Doug Ouellette's
Spider Fly

The flies chosen for this section represent only a few of the patterns used at Pyramid Lake. All come from the fly boxes of veteran Pyramid anglers, most of whom have been fly fishing for Pyramid's cutthroat thirty times or more a season for over 20 years. Their flies and techniques are worth a try anytime you fish the lake, especially when traditional approaches are not producing
Photo: Ann & Ron Privrasky and Ron Anfinson.

Black/Black with Red Tail Woolly Worm

Hook: Mustad 3906B or 9672/TMC 3761 or 5262 sizes 2 to 8.
Thread: Black 6/0.
Tail: Red marabou pinched to 1/2 to 1/3 body length.
Body: Black medium or large chenille.
Hackle: Two to 4 black saddle hackles of appropriate size tied in tips first. Some tiers still like to tie their hackles in by the butts, but I prefer to tie hackles on my Woolly Worm by the tips.

This pattern has produced more fish for me than any other, including two brutes over 30 inches that were landed and released in about 2 hours.

Rainbow/Black Woolly Worm

Hook: Mustad 3906B or 9672/TMC 3761 or 5262 sizes 2 to 8.
Thread: Black 6/0.
Tail: None.
Body: Rainbow sparkle braid.
Hackle: Black.

When people first look at the Rainbow/Black Woolly Worm, I detect disbelief. With its skinny body and uneven flared hackle, it looks like the product of a beginning fly tying class. Judged on appearance alone, it's hard to have confidence in this pattern, but this scraggly looking fly has made a believer out of a lot of anglers. It's one of those rare color combinations that seem to produce on bright as well as overcast days.

Black/Black/Pearl Wing Woolly Worm

Hook: Mustad 3906B or 9672/TMC 3761 or 5262 sizes 2 to 8.
Thread: Black 6/0.
Tail: None.
Body: Medium to large black chenille.
Hackle: Black.
Wing: Seven to 9 strands of pearl crystal hair.

Purple/Purple/Pearl Wing Woolly Worm

Hook: Mustad 3906B or 9672/TMC 3761 or 5262 sizes 2 to 8.
Thread: Black or purple 6/0.
Tail: None.
Body: Medium to large purple chenille.
Hackle: Purple saddle hackles of appropriate size.
Wing: Seven to 9 strands of pearl crystal hair.

Pink/White Woolly Worm

Hook: Mustad 3906B or 9672/TMC 376 or 5262 sizes 2 to 8.
Thread: White 6/0.
Tail: None.
Body: Med. fluorescent pink chenille, or pink Estaz.
Hackle: Two white saddles of appropriate size.

Chartreuse/White Woolly Worm

Hook: Mustad 3906B or 9672/TMC 3761 or 5262 sizes 2 to 8.
Thread: White 6/0.
Tail: None.
Body: Chartreuse Estaz or medium fluorescent chartreuse chenille.
Hackle: White.

Pearl Estaz/White Woolly Worm

Hook: Mustad 3906B or 9672/TMC 3761 or 5262 sizes 2 to 8.
Thread: White 6/0.
Tail: None.
Body: Pearl Estaz.
Hackle: White.

Variations of the above patterns have also proven effective at Pyramid. A black bodied Woolly Worm with grizzly hackle and red tail is a good combination as is an olive chenille body with grizzly hackle and red tail. An old favorite of some Pyramid anglers is a white chenille body with white hackle and red tail.

Sash Nakamoto, Reno resident and Pyramid fly fishing fanatic, likes to dye his own materials, creating original color combinations for his flies. One of his favorite flies is a cross between a Woolly Worm and Woolly Bugger with a golden-olive-dyed crystal chenille body. As I recommended earlier, Sash makes sure to wrap this pattern with 3 to 4 grizzly hackles dyed the same golden olive color.

The combinations go on and on, but these 7 patterns have the Woolly Worm color combinations I use the most.

Patterns From The Nevada Experts
Pyramid Lake Flies Developed, Tied and Tested by Reno-Area Fly Fishers.

Dave Stanley's Dragon Fly Nymph

Hook: TMC 200, size 6.
Thread: Olive 6/0.
Tail: Olive dyed teal flank.
UnderBody: Olive furry foam.
Dubbing: Light olive hare's ear.
Shellback: Turkey wing quill, dyed olive brown.
Rib: Fine gold wire.
Legs: Same as tail.
Wingcase: Same as shellback.
Eyes: Small glass or bead chain.

This fly rides hook up, so put the hook in the vise upside down. To form the fly's abdomen, tie in teal for the tail, about 3/8 inch long. Next, tie in the turkey quill and gold wire followed by a thin strip of the olive furry foam. Wrap the furry foam around the hook to form a fat abdomen approximately 1/2 inch long. Return the thread back to the point where the tail was tied in, make a dubbing loop with light olive hare's ear, spin loop, and wrap forward to the end of the abdomen. Pull the turkey quill forward, forming the shellback, and tie off. Rib with fine gold wire.

Before beginning the thorax of the fly, tie in the eyes just behind the eye of the hook on the bottom of the shank. Now begin the thorax by tying in the turkey quill for the wingcase against the abdomen, followed by the teal for the legs. Next, tie in another length of furry foam and build up the thorax, keeping it smaller than the abdomen. Wrap the thread back to the turkey quill, form another dubbing loop with light olive hare's ear, wrap it forward and tie off in front of the eyes. Pull the turkey quill for the wingcase forward, tie off, whip finish and cement.

Late winter and early spring, when dragon fly nymphs become active, Stanley has lots of success with this fly. He casts an intermediate line into rocky areas along Pyramid's shoreline. He usually uses his dragonfly nymph as the point fly with a black or purple Woolly Worm as the dropper.

Mark Tilton's Tui Chub Streamer

Hook: Mustad 9674 ring eye, TMC 200R
sizes 4 to 6
Thread: White 6/0.
Tail: Loose mylar strands.
Body: Mylar tape folded over hook shank and shaped, covered with medium chartreuse mylar.
Under Wing: Pearl Flash-a-bou.
Middle Wing: Chartreuse crystal flash.
Top Wing: Peacock sword.
Head: White thread with painted eyes.

After securing the hook in the vise, cut a piece of mylar tape about a shank length long and approximately 2/3 the depth of the gap. Next, fold it over the hook, then trim to the shape of a minnow. Secure the tying thread to the rear of the hook, but do not bring it forward beyond the barb. Prepare the mylar tubing, slide it over the formed minnow body, tie the tubing down even with the barb of hook, whip finish, and cut thread. Trim the frayed ends of the mylar tubing, leaving about 1/4 body length for the tail.

To finish, restart the thread 2 eye-lengths behind the eye of the hook. Tie down the front end of the mylar tubing and closely trim the loose ends. At this point, tie in 10 to 12 strands of Flash-a-bou for the underwing, a dozen strands of crystal flash to form the middle wing, and 12 strands of Peacock Sword for the topping. Extend the tips of all three to the end of the tail. Finally, form a large, bullet-shaped head and whip finish. After several coats of head cement, paint black eyes on each side of head. After the eyes have dried completely, finish with several more coats of head cement.

Tilton says this pattern is most effective in early fall and late spring when large numbers of tui chub congregate in the shallows. It's an excellent producer most other times of the year as well. Using steady, 8 to 10 inch strips, he fishes this fly with an intermediate shooting head on a 7 1/2 foot tapered leader with an 8 to 10 pound tippet.

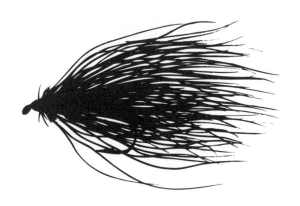

Doug Ouellette's Spider Fly

Hook: Mustad 3906B size 4.
Thread: Black 6/0.
Body/Tail: Palmered purple marabou tied in butt first, followed by palmered black marabou. Only the front half of hook is used.

Doug recomends using a Hi-Speed, Hi-D shooting head with a white or pink Woolly Worm dropper. With the Spider Fly tied on the point, you'll have an excellent producer. "Cutthroat seem to inhale flies, and sometimes these takes go undetected. The light weight Spider Fly helps you feel these subtle strikes. The undulating marabou on this fly is irresistible to Pyramid's large fish."

Glenn Allred's Hard body Sculpin

Hook: Partridge Carrie Steven's Streamer Hook 10X long, or Mustad 9575 sizes 4 and 6.
Thread: Black 6/0.
Tag: Small silver mylar about 5 to 7 turns depending on hook size.
Tail: Black dyed mink or rabbit (brown or olive can be substituted).
UnderBody: Black embroidery thread or floss wrapped over sewing pins with points cut off and attached to sides of hook with pin heads facing forward to taper body.
Abdomen: Clear Body Glass or Larva Lace over a lateral line of silver tinsel and a trimmed and cemented feather (ring necked pheasant "church window," speckled hen back feather, or grizzly hackle).
Wing: Same as tail with tips reaching to end of tail.

Throat: Wine color dyed rabbit with tips reaching to hook point.
Thorax: Dyed black, brown, or olive spun deer hair trimmed slightly flat on top and bottom and flared slightly on sides.
Head: Shaped in traditional bullet-head style. White with black pupils are preferred colors for painted eyes.

The abdomen is the only tricky part of this pattern. After the underbody is satisfactorily tapered (thin at the end and thick at the forward 2/3 of the hook), take the thread back to the tail and tie in the Body Glass, the silver tinsel on each side of the abdomen for the lateral lines, and the trimmed and cemented feather of choice on top. Next, bring the thread to the front of the abdomen, and pull the silver tinsel forward on each side of the abdomen to form the lateral lines, and tie off. Now, pull the trimmed and cemented feather forward over everything, and again tie off. Cover the abdomen with close wraps of Body Glass, tie off, epoxy, let dry.

Obviously, this fly is for advanced tiers. To learn more about "hardbody" flies, try *The Master Fly Weaver* by George F. Grant. He originated these types of patterns.

Depending on the wind at Pyramid, Allred uses this pattern as the point fly on a 9 to 12 foot leader tapering to a 6 to 8 pound test tippet of about 4 feet. Where the tippet joins the leader, he attaches a small bright fly of any design or pattern on a 4 to 6 inch dropper.

Allred likes to use this pattern because of the definite way fish hit it. He retrieves it with short, quick strips, paying close attention as the fly comes over a ledge and again when the dropper fly comes into view before preparing for his next cast.

Ike Berry's Foam Beetle

Hook: Tiemco 2457 size 10.
Thread: Brown 8/0.
Body: Jay Fairs' Ugly Bug dubbing or black dubbing, both work equally well.
Shellback: Tan Scintilla foam colored with a dark brown, waterproof marker.

After starting the thread, tie in the foam for the shellback as far past the barb as possible. Next, apply the dubbing material to the thread and wrap forward to build the body, leaving enough room to tie off the foam behind the eye. Pull the foam forward, tie off, and trim the excess, leaving a short tag of the foam for a head. Finally, whip finish and dot the foam with the waterproof marker.

Berry always fishes this beetle pattern as the dropper behind a Woolly Worm or streamer. Preferring 8 pound Maxima for both his tippet and relatively long, 8 inch dropper, he likes to use a short, 6 foot leader with the dropper tied in about 24 inches above the point.

"Don't be afraid to fish Pyramid with small flies," claims Berry. "During certain times of the year, I've seen 8 to 10 pound fish come to the surface for a fly as small as a Griffith's Gnat." Berry reasons that Pyramid's wave action creates riffles on its sandy bottom. These riffles can catch larger hooks and make it difficult for an angler to detect strikes. For this reason, Berry prefers fishing Pyramid with small flies, usually size 10. As an example, his small beetle pattern, tied to a long dropper, floats just a few inches above Pyramid's sand riffles and ledges. With retrieves unimpeded by "false" strikes, Berry feels confident that anything he detects is most likely a fish. This confidence dramatically increases his hook-ups and fish landed.

Berry's preference for smaller carries over to gear. He used to fish big rods because he wanted maximum casting distance. After years of being tired out by heavy tackle, he realized most of the fish he was hooking were within 40 to 50 feet of where he was casting. Departing from the usual Pyramid set-up, Berry now fishes 9 1/2 foot rods for 5 or 6 weight lines. His favorite line is the relatively light Teeny 130. He says this sized-down tackle is adequate for the distances he casts and it has almost completely eliminated the fatigue associated with fishing big tackle at Pyramid.

Berry's lighter gear and smaller flies are certainly one way to go at Pyramid. His small beetle pattern keeps him above the sand, enabling him to detect more strikes, especially when the fish are gently sucking in the fly.

Dragon Nymphs

Tui Chub Zonker

Tui Chub

Mark Tilton's Tui Chub Streamer

Glenn Allred's Hard Body Sculpin

Some Pyramid Lake cutthroat trout food and the immitations used by fly anglers.

Pyramid Lake Preparations

For Fly Fishers Planning A Trip To The Lake

Fishing Regulations

The Pyramid Lake Paiute Tribe sells permits for a wide range of activities at the lake. As of this writing, a "day use" permit (to visit the lake) is $5 per day, a fishing license costs $6 per day. A seasonal permit is $32, and is good from October 1 through June 30. Anglers fishing from boats also need permits which cost the same for a day, or season, as fishing permits. Camping permits run $5 per day. Long-term camping permits are available.

The current fishing regulations at Pyramid Lake permit only artificial lures, meaning flies, spoons, etc. The daily limit is 2 fish. The legal size or slot limits falls between 16 and 19 inches or over 24 inches. Only one fish over 24 inches is allowed in possession. No fish less than 16 inches or between 19 and 24 inches is allowed in possession. Always check current regulations before fishing or boating at Pyramid.

Size and catch limits at Pyramid have been in place since 1991. As the Paiute tribe says, "Consider catch and release, we encourage conservation". Photo: Terry Barron

Annual creel summary information is compiled from information collected from people like you who stop at the Pyramid Lake Creel Census Station. The station is on State Route 445 next to the Pyramid Lake Store. The station, unfortunately, does not have fixed hours so many fish are harvested and never reported. In fact, only about 15% of Pyramid's fishing is reflected by census station information. Needless to say, every angler should make it a point to stop and report fish caught, kept or, preferably, released. This data is crucial to the management of the fishery.

Camping

Whether sightseeing or fishing, camping at Pyramid is one of the most enjoyable ways to experience the lake. With the appropriate permit, you can camp anywhere around the lake that's accessible, and, trust me, "accessible" is tricky. When driving on the shoreline avoid the soft sand. It can suck down even the best four-wheel-drive vehicles. The saying goes, "you're not a true resident of Nevada unless you've been stuck in the sand at Pyramid."

A hard-sided recreational vehicle insures a pleasant camping experience at Pyramid, even during the fierce snowstorms which can hit the lake from September through May. Tent campers better make sure their shelter can withstand high winds and be prepared for cold weather, even in the warm

Camping at Pyramid is best done in an RV of some kind. Solitude or groups are available.   Photo: Terry Barron.

summer months. Small campfires are usually allowed, though I'd check at the ranger station to be sure. Camping on Pyramid's vast shoreline helps anglers get into the water in a matter of minutes. You'll also get the chance to witness the sunrise.

Signs on state route 445 and The Pyramid Lake Store. Venerable land marks on the way to the lake when coming from Reno. Photos: Terry Barron.

Accommodations & Services

If the one small motel at the Pyramid is full, and camping is not your cup of tea, ample accommodations in the cities of Reno and Sparks are a mere 30 to 45 minutes from the lake. In addition to the huge hotels and casinos in these resort cities, there are many smaller, affordable motels and hotels. See the appendix for contact numbers.

There is a store, small motel and other services for the angler and sightseer on the west shore of Pyramid Lake. Photo: Terry Barron.

Crosby's Lodge
(At Pyramid Lake)
Sutcliffe, Nevada 89502
702-476-0400

Crosby's is the only lodging at the lake. This 9 unit motel has a small bar and general store with gas, frozen goods, flies and fishing tackle. Permits are not available.

Pyramid Lake Store & Cutthroat Charters
(On the way to the lake)
29555 Pyramid Lake Road
Sutcliffe, Nevada 89502
702-476-0555

Wilbur Smith, and Carla and George Molino own and operate this handy and well-stocked general store and gas station. It's just inside the reservation border on the Pyramid Lake Highway. In addition to a variety of food and drink, the store sells flies, lures, and all permits necessary. I highly recommend their fishing charter service. These are very nice people, and they know a great deal about fishing Pyramid.

Pyramid Lake Marina
Sutcliffe, Nevada 89502
702-476-1156

The main ranger station for Pyramid Lake where all permits can be purchased. This modern building includes a general store with gas and some fishing tackle, RV park with full hook-ups and dump station, boat launch and museum.

Pyramid-Tahoe Fishing Charters
702-852-3474

Captain Lex Moser is the only non-native fishing guide working at Pyramid Lake. He is knowledgeable, well-equipped and comes highly recommended.

Pyramid Lake Marina   *Photo: Terry Barron.*

Fly Tackle and Supplies

The Gilly Fishing Store
1111 N Rock Blvd.
Sparks, Nevada 89431
702-358-6113

A great general and fly fishing tackle store with good Pyramid fishing advice and permits.

Mark Fore and Strike
490 Kietzke Lane
Reno, Nevada 89509
702-322-9559

A large, well-stocked sporting goods and fly fishing tackle store with good Pyramid fishing advice and permits.

Reno Fly Shop
294 East Moana Lane, #14
Reno, Nevada 89502
702-825-3474

The oldest full-line fly shop in Nevada. The area's most complete selection of Pyramid tackle and flies and expert advice. Permits available.

The marina also has a store and interesting museum highlighting Pyramid Lake history and area flora, fauna and sights.   *Photo: Terry Barron.*

R.V. facilities at the Pyramid Lake R.V. park.
            Photo: Terry Barron.

Appendix

Pyramid Lake Region Fly Tackle

Nevada

Reno Fly Shop
(702) 825-3474
294 E. Moana Lane #14
Reno, NV 89502

Pyramid Lake Store
(702) 476-0555
29555 Pyramid Lake Road
Reno, NV 89510

Mark Fore & Strike
Sporting Goods
(702) 322-9559
490 Kietzke Lane
Reno, NV 89502

The Gilly Fishing Store
(702) 358-6113
1111 Rock Blvd.
Sparks, NV 89431

Angler's Edge
(702)782-4734
1589 US Highway 395 S.
Gardnerville, NV 89410

Nevada Jim's Outdoor
Sports
(702) 753-5467
600 Commercial Street
Elko, NV 89801

"Reel Outfitters" at
Rio Suite Hotel & Casino
(702) 247-7883
3700 W. Flamingo Road
Las Vegas, NV 89103

ClearWater Flyfishing
(702) 388-1022
3031 E. Charleston Road #D
Las Vegas, NV 89104

Tahoe Area

Ralph & Lisa Cutter's
California School
of Flyfishing
1(800) 58TROUT
PO Box 8212
Truckee, CA 96162

Mountain Hardware
(916) 582-4844
11320 Donner Pass Rd.
Truckee, CA 96161

Truckee River Outfiters
April-Oct. (530) 582-0900
Oct.-April (702) 825-3474
10200 Donner Pass Road
Truckee, CA 96161

Tahoe Fly Fishing Outfitters
(916) 541-8208
3433 Lake Tahoe Blvd.
South Lake Tahoe, CA 96150

California Foothills

Nevada City Anglers
(916) 478-9301
417 Broad St.
Nevada City, CA 95959

Mother Lode Angler
(916) 272-3474
13683 Day Road
Grass Valley, CA 95945

Mother Lode Fly Shop
(209) 532-8600
14841 Mono Way
E. Sonora, CA 95327

White Pines Outdoors
(209) 795-1054
2132 Highway 4
Arnold, CA

High Sierra Flyfisher
(760) 375-5810
337 W. Ridgecrest Blvd.
Ridgecrest, CA 93555

Yosemite Creek Outfitters
(209) 962-5060
18729 Main Street - B
Groveland, CA 95321

Northern California

The Fly Shop
1(800) 669-3474
4140 Churn Creek Road
Redding, CA 96002

Sportsman's Den
(916) 283-2733
1580East Main Street
Quincy, CA 95971

Gold Rush Sporting Goods
(916) 832-5724
280 E. Sierra Street
Portola, CA 96122

Kiene's Fly Shop
(916) 486-9958
2654 Marconi Ave.
Sacramento, CA 95821

Fly Fishing Specialties #1
(916) 366-9252
9500 Micron Ave. #129
Sacramento, CA 95827

Fly Fishing Specialties #2
(916) 722-1055
6412-C Tupelo Drive
Citrus Heights, CA 95621

Grizzly Country Store
(916) 832-0270
Lake Davis Road
Portola, CA 96100

Upstream Fly Fishing
(650) 462-1603
552 Waverly Street
Palo Alto, CA 94301

San Francisco Area

Fly Fishing Outfitters
(415) 781-3474
463 Bush Street
San Francisco, CA 94108

Orvis San Francisco
(415) 392-1600
300 Grant Ave.
San Francisco, CA 94108

Southern California

Bell's Sporting Goods
& Hardware
(619) 647-6406
Lee Vining, CA 93541

Ken's Alpine Shop &
Sporting Goods
(619) 932-7707
258 Main Street
Bridgeport, CA 93517

Trout Fitter
(619) 924-3676
Shellmart # 3
Mammoth Lakes, CA
93546

Yosemite Angler
(209) 966-8377
49er Shopping Center
Mariposa, CA 95350

Village Sport Shop
(209) 372-1286
Yosemite Park, CA 1209-372

Buz's Fly & Tackle
(209) 734-1151
400 N. Johnson Ave.
Visalia, CA 93291

Range of Light Outfitters
(209) 635-1500
2020 W. Whitendale Road
Visalia, CA 93277

San Diego Fly Shop
(619) 283-3445
4401 Twain Ave. #6
San Diego, CA 92120

Bob Marriott's
(714) 525-1827
2700 W. Orangethorpe
Fullerton, CA 92633

The Fishermen's Spot
(818) 785-7306
14423 Burbank Blvd.
Van Nuys, CA 91401

Mike Scott's Hackel & Flies
(7140998-9400
2324 N. Batavia #116
Orange, CA 92665

Stroud Tackle
(619) 276-4822
1457 Morena Blvd.
San Diego, CA 92110

Additional Information

Bibliography

Grant, George F.,
The Master Fly Weaver,
Portland, Champoeg Press
p. 230, 1980.

La Rivers, Ira
*Fishes and Fisheries of
Nevada*. Reno, Nevada State
Fish & Game Commission
p. 782, 1962.

Sigler, William
and John Sigler,
*Fishes of the Great Basin: A
Natural History*,
Reno, University of Nevada
Press, p. 425, 1987

Wheeler, S.H.,
*The Desert Lake: The Story
of Nevada's Pyramid Lake*
Caldwell, Idaho, Caxton
Printers Ltd., p. 133, 1974.

Wydoski, R.S.
and R.R. Whitney,
Inland Fishes of Washington,
(sited, Sigler W. & J., *Fishes
of the Great Basin, A Natural
History*)

Clubs & Associations

Truckee River Fly fishers
Call Reno Fly Shop for
current contact number.

Tahoe Truckee Fly Fishers
Call Reno Fly Shop for
current contact number.

Great Basin Bassers
Call the Gilly Fishing Store
for current contact number.

Trout Unlimited (Elko)
Call Nevada Jim's for
current contact number.

Las Vegas Fly Fishing Club
2728 Tidewater Court
Las Vegas, NV 89117

The Federation
of Fly Fishers
National Headquarters
(406) 585-7592
Call for local club
www.fedflyfishers.org

National Fresh Water
Fishing Hall of Fame
(715) 634-4440
P.O. Box 33
Hayward, WI 54843

Government Resources, Nevada

Nevada Division of Wildlife
State Headquarters
1100 Valley Rd.
Reno, NV 89520
(702) 688-1500

NDW Region I
380 West "B" St.
Fallon, NV 89406
(702) 423-3171

NDW Region II
1375 Mountain City Highway
Elko, NV 89801
(702) 738-5332

NDW Region III
4747 Vegas Dr.
Las Vegas, NV 89108
(702) 486-5127

Humboldt National Forest
976 Mountain City Hwy
Elko, NV 89801
(702) 738-5171

Nevada State Recreation Areas

South Fork (702) 758-6493

Wild Horse (702) 758-6493

Cave Lake (702) 728-4467

Echo Canyon (702) 962-5103

Lahontan Rsv. (702) 577-2226

Rye Patch Rsv.(702) 538-7321

Floyd Lamb (702) 486-5413

Lake Tahoe (702) 831-0494

Washoe Lake (702) 687-4319

Toiyabe National Forest
1200 Franklin Way
Sparks, NV 89431
(702) 331-6444

Ruby Lake Wildlife Refuge
(702) 779-2237
Box 60-860
Ruby Valley, NV 89833

Cave Lake State Park
(702) 728-4467 (Dist. Hqts.)
P.O. Box 761
Ely, NV 89301

Government Resources, California

California Office of Tourism
(916) 322-1397
801 K St. Suite #1600
Sacramento, CA 95814

Lake Tahoe Forest Service
870 Emerald Bay Road
S. Lake Tahoe, CA 96150
(916) 573-2600

Bureau of Land Management
(916) 978-4754
2800 Cottage Way
Sacramento, CA 95825

United States Forest Service
(415) 705-2874
630 Sansome Street
San Francisco, CA 94111

Other Fly Fishing Resources

Trout Talk
1(800)AM Hatch
Virtual Fly Fishing Radio
Call for stations & times

The Fly Paper
Fly Tying Newsletter
Burkfly Enterprises
2205 Hilltop Drive #150
Redding, CA 96002

NDOW Radio Program
"On the Wildside of Life"

Fishing Conditions
Reno, KKOH AM 780

Minden, KGVM-FM 99.3

Fallon, KVLV-AM 980

Tonopah, KHWK-FM 92.7

Ely, KDSS-FM 93

Winnemucca,

KWNA-AM 1400

References & Other Reading

*Nevada & Northern California
Atlas & Gazetteer*
Delorme Mapping

*Ken Hanley's No Nonsense
Guide to Fly Fishing in
Northern California*
David Communications

*Dave Stanley's No Nonsense
Guide to Fly Fishing
in Nevada*
David Communications

Nevada Angling Guide
Richard Dickerson

California Fly Fisher

Fly Fishing The Internet

www.fedflyfishers.org
www.flyshop.com
www.flyfishamerica.com
www. gofishing.com
www.ffa.com
www.fly-fishing-women.com
www.tu.org/troutor/m/
metolrec/htm
www.flyfishing.com.asf
www.ool.com/fff
www.ohwy.com
www.amrivers.org
www.gorp.com
www.flyfishto.com

Guidebooks
www.amazon.com
www.bookzone.com
www.powells.com
www.booksnow.com
www.justgoodbooks.com
www.adventurous
traveloer.com
www. barnes&noble.com

Air Travel
www. americanair.com
www. alaskaair.com
www. flycontinental.com
www. delta-air.com
www. nwa.com
www. southwest.com
www. ual.com
www. usair.com

Travel Bookings
www.itn.com
www.thetrip.com
www.travelweb.com
www.previewtravel.com

Weigh Your Catch With a Tape Measure

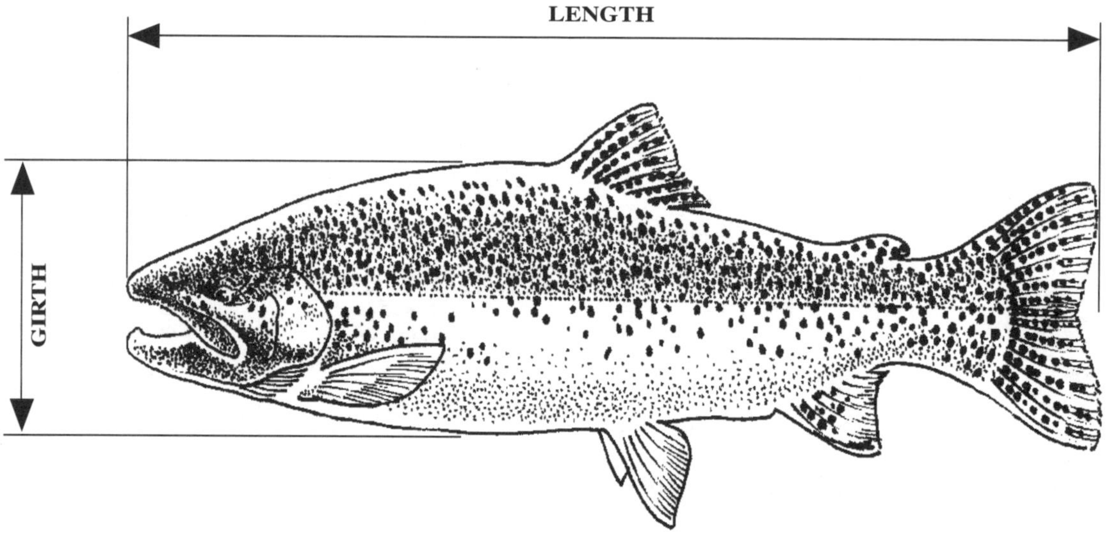

EXAMPLE: A fish 20" long and 14" around (at its thickest part) weighs 4.9 pounds.

Girth (inches)	10	12	14	16	18	20	22	24	26	28	30
8	0.8	1.0	1.1	1.3	1.4	1.6	1.8	1.9	2.1	2.2	2.4
10	1.3	1.5	1.8	2.0	2.3	2.5	2.8	3.0	3.3	3.5	3.8
12	1.8	2.2	2.5	2.9	3.2	3.6	4.0	4.3	4.7	5.0	5.4
14	2.5	2.9	3.4	3.9	4.4	4.9	5.4	5.9	6.4	6.9	7.4
16	3.2	3.8	4.5	5.1	5.8	6.4	7.0	7.7	8.3	9.0	9.6
18	4.1	4.9	5.7	6.5	7.3	8.1	8.9	9.7	10.5	11.3	12.2
20	5.0	6.0	7.0	8.0	9.0	10.0	11.0	12.0	13.0	14.0	15.0

Length (inches)

Tip of nose to notch at the center of tail.

Courtesy of Ralph & Lisa Cutter's California School of Flyfishing • P.O. Box 8212, Truckee, CA 96162 • 1 (800) 58-TROUT

No Nonsense Fly Fishing Knots to Know for Pyramid Lake

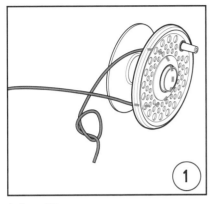 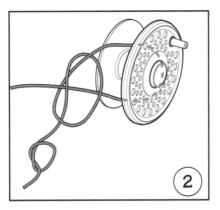 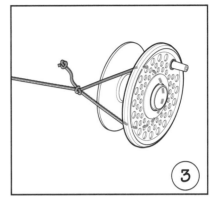

Arbor Knot Use this knot to attach backing to your fly reel. You'll need 100 yards of backing for Pyramid Lake.

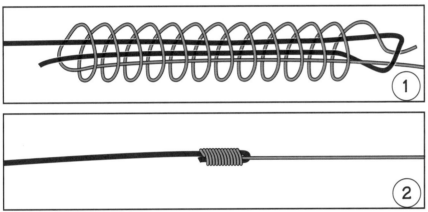

Albright Knot Use this knot to connect backing to the fly line or shooting line

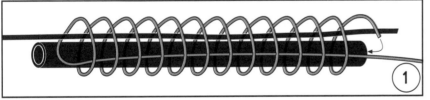

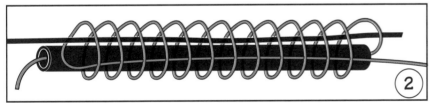

FLY LINE

LEADER

Nail Knot Use a nail, needle or a small tube to tie this knot, which connects the forward end of the fly line to the butt end of the leader. Follow this with a Prefection Loop, and you've got a permanent end loop that allows easy leader changes.

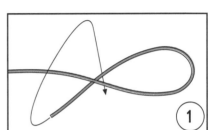

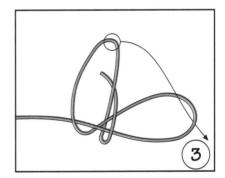

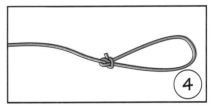

Perfection Loop Use this knot to create a loop in the butt end of the leader. You can easily "loop-to-loop" your leader to your fly line.

No Nonsense Fly Fishing Knots to Know for Pyramid Lake

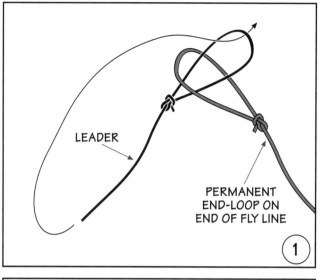

LEADER

PERMANENT END-LOOP ON END OF FLY LINE

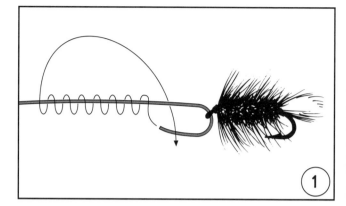

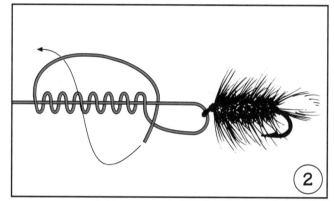

Loop To Loop Use this simple knot to connect the leader to an end loop on the tip of the fly line

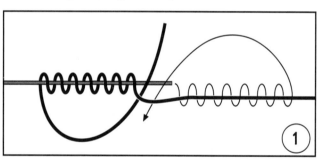

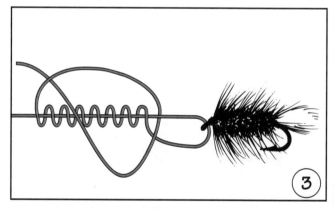

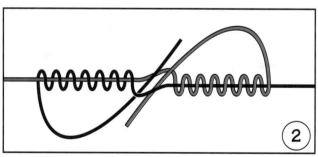

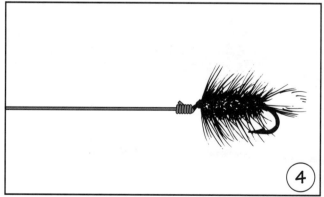

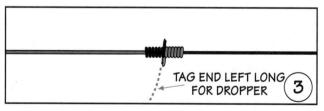

TAG END LEFT LONG FOR DROPPER

Blood Knot Use this knot to connect sections of leader material. To add a dropper, leave the heavier tag end long and attach fly.

Improved Clinch Knot Use this knot to attach a fly to the end of the tippet. Remember to moisten the knot just before you pull it tight.

❖ V ❖

No Nonsense Fly Fishing Knots to Know for Pyramid Lake

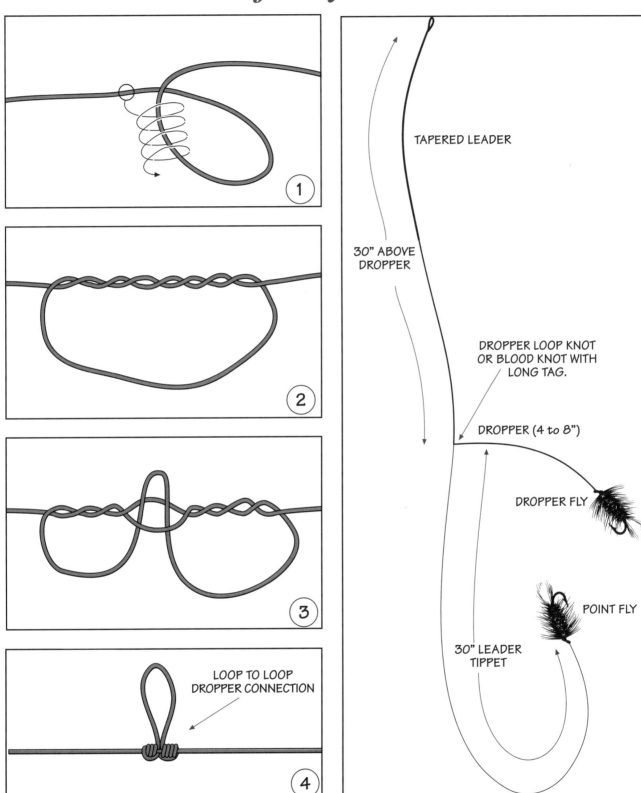

TAPERED LEADER

30" ABOVE DROPPER

DROPPER LOOP KNOT OR BLOOD KNOT WITH LONG TAG.

DROPPER (4 to 8")

DROPPER FLY

POINT FLY

30" LEADER TIPPET

LOOP TO LOOP DROPPER CONNECTION

Dropper Loop Use this knot to attach a dropper to the leader. Tie a Perfection Loop in the end of the dropper tippet and use the loop-to-loop knot or improved clinch knot to connect the two.

Typical two-fly rig Increase your odds of hooking up by using a two-fly rig like this one. This rig helps get the flies down deeper, a real help in Pyramid Lake.

Easy Field Guide
Fly Fishing Terms
Especially for the Beginner

Action adj. Used to describe the relative resistance to bending as you move down the length of a particular fly rod.

Attractor n. A fly designed to look like no life form in particular, but to attract attention and give the impression of something good to eat.

Backing n. A very strong, thin braided line tied to the fly reel and to which you attach the fly line itself.

Barbless adj. A type of hook which doesn't have a barb on the pointed end. Barbless hooks hold if tension is kept on the line by the fisher.

Beadhead adj. Describes a nymph or wetfly which has a small brass or chrome bead placed on the hook ahead of the fly pattern.

Blood Knot n. A knot used to tie tippet material to the end of a leader.

Caddis Fly n. (*Order Trichoptera*) A very common waterborne insect with wings held back and up at a 45 degree angle.

Catch and Release n. The practice of releasing all fish caught with a fly rod unharmed. It is based on a value that the fishing experience is more important than keeping fish.

Char n. (*Salvelinus*) American Brook Trout and Lake Trout are examples of Char found in the United States. Char are cousins of trout, and breed with them, but their offspring are sterile.

Cutthroat Trout n. (*Oncorhynchus clarki*) A trout originally indigenous to the Western drainages of the Rocky Mountains, it is distinguished by red throat slashes under its jaw.

Damselfly n. (*Enallagma cyathigarum*) A large aquatic fly with a long skinny, blue thorax and wings that are held back at an angle.

Disk Drag n. A mechanical method of applying resistance to fly line as it is drawn out by a fish that is hooked.

Dolly Varden n. A Char that often runs to the sea.

Double Haul n. A type of cast characterized by the quick pulling in and releasing of line in both the backcast and the forecast.

Double Taper adj. Describes a fly line that tapers at each end, allowing the user to reverse the line when one end wears out.

Dun n. The stage of a waterborne insect just after it has emerged and has the ability to fly.

Emerger n. That stage in the development of a waterborne insect when it leaves its shuck and emerging into a flying insect.

False Cast v. Casting without ever delivering the fly to the water.

Fly Line n. The thick-bodied line attached to the backing, which is used to actually cast the fly.

Lake Trout n. (*Salvelinus namaycush*) Not real trout, a member of the Char family. They not only live in lakes, they also spawn there.

Leader n. A thin, clear monofilament tapered line attached to the end of the fly line, to which either the tippet or fly is attached.

Loading n. The act of bending a fly rod at the end of a back cast, which is caused by the weight of the fly line transferring its weight into stored energy held in the bent fly rod.

Nymph n. An undeveloped insect. Nymphs live under water for months prior to emerging into a winged insect.

Polarized Sun Glasses n. Vital to the fly-fisher's outfit. Three functions: 1) Allow the fisher to see into the water past the glare from reflected sunlight. 2) Shade eyes from harmful UV rays. 3) Protect eyes from hooks.

Rainbow Trout n. (*Oncorhynchus mykiss*) Indigenous to the Pacific drainages of the Rocky Mountains and known for the rich pinkish colorations along the center line of the fish.

Rest the Water v. Allowing the water to calm after a disturbance.

Roll Cast n. Used where there is little room behind for a backcast.

Run n. A location in a stream characterized by shallow running water over a rocky streambed that feeds into a pool.

Salmon n. A large member of the *salmonidae* fish family which hatch in fresh water and migrate to a lake or the ocean. Some return to the stream of their origin to spawn and then die.

Scud n. A very small cold water crustacean often erroneously referred to as "freshwater shrimp."

Shooting Line v. The act of releasing extra line held in the free hand as the line passes the caster in the forecast.

Shooting Taper n. Used to describe a rather short (45-46 feet) fly line with a majority of the weight out at the front end.

Single Action adj. A fly reel that has fixed drag, set at the factory.

Sink Tip adj. Floating fly line with about ten feet of sinking line built into, or attached to, the front end.

Spinner n. The final stage of a waterborne insect during the mating session, when it falls, fatigued, to the water and dies.

Steelhead n. A type of rainbow trout that migrates from the stream or river in which it is hatched to the ocean or a large landlocked lake.

Stocker adj. A fish born and raised in a hatchery and then placed in a stream, river or lake for sport fishing purposes.

Stonefly n. (*Order Plecoptera*) A large aquatic fly that emerges by crawling out of the water onto a stone or rock and then splits its shuck and becomes a flying insect.

Streamer n. A fly that imitates a small fish, worm, leech, etc.

Strip v. Retrieval of the fly line with the hand not holding the fly rod.

Surgeon's Knot n. Used to attach tippet material to the end of a leader.

Terrestrial n. A fly that imitates insects not waterborne, such as a grasshopper, cricket, ant, or beetle.

Tippet Material n. Very thin, monofilament material added to the end of a leader to extend the length or to rebuild the leader.

Wader Belt n. A stretchable belt worn around the waist of waders, intended to keep the water out should the wearer fall into the water.

Weight n. A system of measuring fly line size from 1 (lightest) to 15 (heaviest) determined by the weight of the first 30 feet of line.

Weight Forward adj. A fly line with more weight toward the front to assist casting.

Wild adj. Fish born in the waters in which they are found, as opposed to hatchery raised fish stocked into their current waters.

Woolly Bugger n. A wet fly that imitates a number of underwater food items fish may be interested in.

"X" Ratings n. A system of describing the approximate thickness of leaders and tippet material. The system runs from 010X (.021 diameter at the tippet = very large) down to 7X (.004 diameter at the tippet = smaller than a human hair).

Definitions from *The Easy Field Guide to Fly-Fishing Terms & Tips* by David Phares. For the complete list of terms, tips and some humor send $2.00 to: Primer Publishers 5738 North Central Avenue Phoenix, Arizona 85012

About
No Nonsense Guides

Harry Teel
Harry Teel's No Nonsense Guide
To Fly Fishing In Central & Southeastern Oregon
The Metolius, Deschutes, McKenzie, Owyhee, John Day and 35 others.

Mr. Teel wrote the first No Nonsense fly fishing guide in 1993. It's been reprinted 4 times and was updated, expanded and improved in 1998.

For the better part of 60 years Mr. Teel fly fished his home state as well as various waters around the world. He and the publisher combined his years of fishing notes into a guidebook.

In the early 80's Harry opened and operated The Fly Fisher's Place, the fly shop in the Central Oregon town of Sisters. He's since retired and pursuers fish and birdies. Jeff Perin, present owner of the shop, provided much new material for the 1998 edition.

Bill Mason
Bill Mason's No Nonsense Guide
To Fly Fishing In Idaho
The Henry's Fork, Salmon, Snake and Silver Creek plus 24 other waters.

Mr. Mason penned the first fly fishing guidebook to Idaho in 1994. It features the best fly fishing waters and showcases Bill's 30 plus years of Idaho fly fishing experience.

Bill helped build a major outfitting operation at the Henry's Fork and helped open the first fly shop in Boise. In Sun Valley he developed the first fly fishing school and guiding program at Snug Fly Fishing, a fly shop he operated for 15 years. Bill eventually purchased the shop, renaming it Bill Mason Sun Valley Outfitters which has served fly fishers for over 20 years.

Jackson Streit
Jackson Streit's No Nonsense Guide
To Fly Fishing In Colorado
The Colorado, Rio Grande, Platte, Gunnison, Mountain lakes and more.

Mr. Streit has fly fished in Colorado for over 27 years. This vast experience was condensed into the third No Nonsense fly fishing guidebook, published in 1995 and updated, improved and reprinted in 1997.

In 1971 Jackson started the first guide service in the Breckenridge area. In 1985 he opened the region's first fly shop, The Mountain Angler, which he owns and manages.

Mr. Streit has fly fished the western United States, many countries and various tropical islands. He's written numerous fly fishing articles and is involved in many Trout Unlimited activities.

Ken Hanley
Ken Hanley's No Nonsense Guide
To Fly Fishing In Northern California
The Sacramento, Hat Creek, Russian, resevoirs, saltwater and bass on a fly.

Mr. Hanley has fished all the waters in this guide. While traveling the world and leading adventure expeditions he's caught over 50 species of gamefish. He's also written much on the subject including three other books.

Ken writes outdoor related pieces for a variety of magazines and newspapers. This highly enthusiastic speaker and tier is sought by fly fishing clubs, expositions and trade shows.

Taylor Streit
Taylor Streit's No Nonsense Guide
To Fly Fishing In New Mexico
The San Juan, Cimarron, Gila, Chama, Rio Grand, mountain lakes and more.

The first all inclusive guide to the top fly fishing waters in the "Land of Enchantment". Since 1970 Taylor has been *THE* New Mexico fly fishing authority and #1 professional guide. He's also developed many fly patterns used throughout the region. Taylor owned the Taos Fly Shop for ten years and managed a bone fishing lodge in the Bahamas. He makes winter fly fishing pilgrimages to Argentina where he escorts fly fishers and explores.

Dave Stanley
Dave Stanley's No Nonsense Guide
To Fly Fishing In Nevada
The Truckee, Walker, Carson, Eagle, Davis, Ruby, mountain lakes and more.

Mr. Stanley is recognized nationwide as the most knowledgeable fly fisher and outdoorsman in the state of Nevada. He also travels throughout the west and other warm climes where he leads fly fishing excursions. He own's and operates the Reno Fly Shop and a satellite shop in Truckee, California. His life of fly angling and Nevada experience combines into a must read guidebook to Nevada's secluded waters.

The guide's talented coauthor, **Jeff Cavender**, is a Nevada native and manager of the Reno Fly Shop. Jeff teaches fly casting and tying. He's taught and guided all over Nevada and California during the past 30 + years. Jeff provided direction and edited Terry Barron's Pyramid Lake guidebook.

Where No Nonsense Guides Come From

No Nonsense guidebooks give a quick, clear, understanding of the essential information needed to fly fish a region's most outstanding waters. The authors are highly experienced and qualified local fly fishers. Maps are tidy versions of the authors sketches.

These guides are produced by the fly fishers, their friends, and spouses of fly fishers, at David Communications. The publisher is located in the tiny Western town of Sisters, Oregon, just a few miles from the Metolius River.

All who produce No Nonsense guides believe in providing top quality products at a reasonable price. We also believe all information should be verified. We never hesitate to go out, fly rod in hand, to verify the facts and figures that appear in the pages of these guides. The staff is committed to this research. It's dirty work, but we're glad to do it for you.

The illustrations and maps in these books are the work of Pete Chadwell. As a fly fisherman, Pete is more than happy to apply his considerable drawing talents to things that live and float in and on water. His detailed maps are a testimony to his desire for accuracy and to get out and fly fish new waters.

The computer work and design of No Nonsense guides is the work of Aprille Chadwell. Aprille's firm, Dynamic Arts, provides graphic art services for a variety of clients. She was dragged into producing No Nonsense fly fishing guides by the publisher and her husband.

Look for new No Nonsense Fly Fishing guides to other important regions!

NEVADA HIGHWAY NETWORK

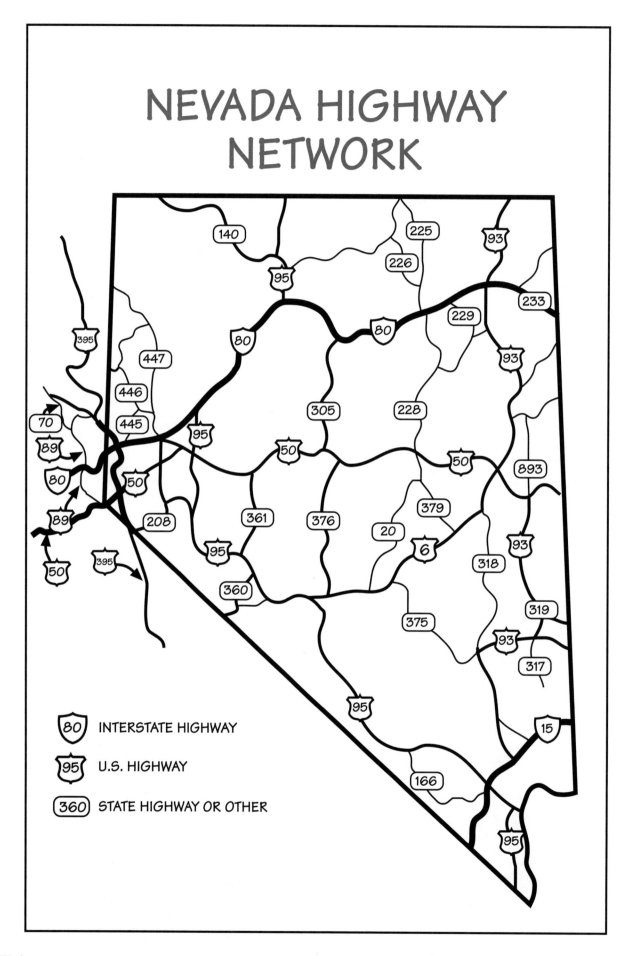